James and his team support my community with financial advice to live their best lives. He is a genius in this space and this book gives away all his secrets.

**Victoria Devine, founder of**
**#1 finance podcast *She's on the Money***

People say, 'Never judge a book by its cover.' Well this great book is the exact antidote of that. Look again at that cover. And judge it. And when you read it, you'll find that it's clearly different than the 'normal' wealth book. It takes you on the journey of a lifetime — very specifically YOUR lifetime. And your lifetime becomes an even better one — simply because you read and than acted on the stunning advice inside.

**Paul Dunn, Chairman B1G1: Business for Good,**
**4 times TEDx speaker and best-selling author**

James has cracked the code in making financial advice relatable, approachable and insanely valuable for young people. Read the book, follow the 5x D's and achieve your version of 'sufficient funds'.

**Glen James, author and founder of the**
***this is money* podcast**

T0335188

# INSUFFICIENT FUNDS

# INSUFFICIENT FUNDS

## MAKE THE RIGHT MONEY DECISIONS
### TO BRING YOUR BIG PLANS TO LIFE

## JAMES MILLARD

WILEY

First published in 2024 by John Wiley & Sons Australia, Ltd
Level 4, 600 Bourke St, Melbourne, Victoria 3000, Australia

Typeset in Plantin Std Regular 11.5pt/15.5pt

© James and Natascha Millard and related entities 2024

The moral rights of the author have been asserted

ISBN: 978-1-394-24889-6

NATIONAL
LIBRARY
OF AUSTRALIA

A catalogue record for this
book is available from the
National Library of Australia

Cover design by Wiley
Cover Image: © DisobeyArt/Adobe Stock
Finance icons (figure 2.2, p69): © Icons-Studio / Adobe Stock

**Disclaimer**

The material in this publication is of the nature of general comment only, and does not represent professional advice. It is not intended to provide specific guidance for particular circumstances and it should not be relied on as the basis for any decision to take action or not take action on any matter which it covers. Readers should obtain professional advice where appropriate, before making any such decision. To the maximum extent permitted by law, the author and publisher disclaim all responsibility and liability to any person, arising directly or indirectly from any person taking or not taking action based on the information in this publication.

*\*\*\**

The information contained in this book is general in nature and does not take into account your personal situation. Before acting on any information, you should consider the appropriateness of the information for your objectives, financial situation and needs.

All client names and a bunch of other identifying details have been changed in this book for privacy reasons.

*To Tash, thank you for co-writing this book with me and the stories within. Love you.*

*To Ada and Eden, you make Mum and Dad so proud. This one's for you.*

\*\*\*

*We acknowledge the Awabakal people, the traditional custodians of the lands on which we live and work, and where this book was written. We acknowledge the cultural diversity of all Aboriginal and Torres Strait Islander peoples and pay respect to Elders past, present and future.*

# CONTENTS

# INTRODUCTION

*Insufficient Funds* is a super-common and very relatable concept. In fact, almost all of us know it a little too well.

Whether you've been abruptly confronted by this problem at a checkout or an ATM, or have suffered the rude shock of being unprepared for a financial emergency, or it's just a general feeling you get when you think about your money, you're familiar with the discomfort it brings. Insufficient Funds is a place you've been — there's a good chance you're there right now and that's why you picked up this book.

The scary thing is that, if left unaddressed, this predicament can ruin you. It can dampen your motivation, crush your lust for life and smother your chances of achieving all the good things you were born to achieve. If left to fester for too long, it can see you settling for a lesser life than the one you're capable of living, and ending up unhappy and unfulfilled.

As you begin to read this book, more than likely your starting point is Insufficient Funds, as defined by you. Crucially, this will not always be obvious. You may not be swimming in debt or have a $0 bank account. Perhaps it's just a feeling that you're not on track, or you find yourself comparing your life to your friends' or family's, and wishing it was different. It could be you're not happy with your financial progress or direction, you're overwhelmed by options and decision fatigue. Perhaps you're uncertain about how your current financial decisions will impact your and your family's future.

My goal in this book is to guide you far away from this place and ensure you never return.

# The true meaning of Sufficient Funds

Most people we meet in our financial advice business are struggling to align their money decisions with their lives in a way that ensures they have 'sufficient funds'. Often this is because they haven't defined *sufficient* as it applies to them and therefore are chasing their tails. Even if they have a financial plan, it's destined to fail if they haven't stopped and asked themselves the all-encompassing question: *What really matters to me?*

We all strive for financial wellbeing. While this will look different for each of us, essentially it could be defined as 'having sufficient funds for your chosen lifestyle at a given point in time'.

Sufficient Funds doesn't mean being restricted to a low-cost, meagre existence and just getting by. Sufficient for you is about defining what your ideal life looks like then creating and implementing a plan to make it happen!

This involves giving yourself permission to give society's norms the big middle finger. For too long society's expectations have set the rules for us: get an education, get a job, get married, buy a house, have kids, work 9 to 5 for 40 years, take two to four weeks' holiday a year, retire ... then die. Not cool. Life should be way more fun than this!

Life isn't like golf where the quality of the dot points don't matter and the only thing that counts is the number on the card at the end of the game. You could land one shot in the water, the next in the bunker and still sink one from 100 metres out for par. Our lives are defined by the time we spend between the dots, not the scorecard. You make micro money decisions every single day, but do you ever stop to think about the impact of these decisions on the life you're striving for?

Your ability to live the life you dream of is dictated by two core components:

1. making sound financial decisions

2. aligning these decisions with your ideal life.

In our work, we meet lots of people who have a fairly good handle on number 1, but almost no one truly gets the second part. Sound financial decisions mean little in the long run if you're not happy. So these two elements go very much hand in hand. You need to be able to cut through to the core of what makes you tick, then be strategic about how you put it all in place. It's tough, but I'm about to show you how.

I spend my days helping people see what's possible with their finances and in this book I'm going to share all this with you and more. It's time to live on your own terms, with a good stash of cash to create *your* dream life, whatever that means to you.

Let's roll on and see how you're going to take your life from Insufficient to Sufficient Funds.

# The ATM slip and one all-time road trip

At 20 years old, during my time at university, I was lucky enough to do a semester in Canada. I studied for four months at UVic on Vancouver Island in BC. I surfed in a 5mm wetsuit in 6-degree water, had a season pass at Whistler, partied five nights a week, and passed all of my subjects with flying colours (read: a consistent 50 per cent!). I made friends for life with a bunch of peeps who had a lust for living the likes of which I'd never seen. Maybe it was the mountains, or the Fireball! At the end of that semester I met up with G-Rod, Sammy and Jezza, three of my best mates from home who had also been 'studying' in North America, and we pulled off a dream road trip on a shoestring budget.

A few weeks before we left on this adventure we'd been out drinking at Customs House, one of the usual hangs in Newcastle. It was student-night $1 drinks, four at a time—a standard Wednesday really for campus-living uni students. One of the boys, who had sold his body board for $40 just to come out for a night, returned from the ATM with 'Insufficient Funds' obtrusively highlighted on his receipt. We all lost it! But as the laughter died a terrible idea was hatched. Insufficient Funds would be an awesome band name! Jezza had mad skills on the piano, but given the rest of us had little to offer in the way of musical talent we reluctantly concluded that this wasn't going to be our path to fame and fortune. The Customs' drinks flowed and the plans continued to gain momentum. We would start a surf brand instead! A week later we had 50 trucker caps and T-shirts with Insufficient Funds printed and we sold these to our mates, as well as a few on eBay. We were gaining notoriety around the Newcastle Uni campus. Fuelled by the dream of our future multimillion-dollar baby, we flew out on our overseas exchange with grand visions of surfing, travelling and partying without strings.

For a thousand bucks US we bought a beat-up old Chrysler LeBaron station wagon, the one with the wooden panels. It was a shocker, so luckily for us we had our accents for currency. We drove this beast around the US for two months, covering 10 865 miles across 18 states. We basically tracked a horseshoe from Vancouver, Canada, down the west coast to Baja, Mexico, over to Florida, up to Ontario, Canada, and back to New York City. We dumped the car in the Bronx — keys in the ignition — and flew home. The car was registered in Sammy's name and years later his poor mum was still getting holding and towing fines in the mail from Yonkers Police Department. Sorry Louise.

The road trip was long, the tales we still tell even longer. Here are a few (more or less PC) highlights:

- bungee jumping in Nanaimo, Vancouver Island — free on Valentine's Day if you went nude

- the Southern Oregon coast — one of my favourite places in the world: surfing with sea lions chased in by the great whites on a remote beach near Florence, and scaring the shit out of a local fisherman in the process

- Yosemite, CA — hiking and teaming up with a couple of locals who cooked us our first barbecued steaks in months (shout-out to Kevin and Sheldon, who then poured all the leftover blood and meat juices around our tent in the hope we'd experience the local grizzlies up close and personal)

- all the natural wonders — from General Sherman in Sequoia National Park, one of the tallest trees in the world, to Grand Canyon and Sedona in Arizona

- surfing famed California breaks like Steamer Lane and Trestles, and many lesser-known remote spots in Oregon, Cali and Baja, Mexico

- renting kayaks (and scoring bonus joints) from a guy in La Bufadora on the Baja coast, and spending the next five hours exploring the blowhole and random caves — Sammy losing his sunnies and thongs while trying to ride the 'rapids'

- driving through Death Valley, CA, with no aircon, where a flat tyre meant the boys changing the flat in 52-degree heat while I was busy fertilising the cacti as a result of severe food poisoning (thanks Mexico!)

- turning 21 in Vegas — enough said

- partying with a 60-year-old pimp named Al Jolly in Dallas, TX

- riding bikes, dodging snakes and massive gators, around the Everglades

- ending up on the 'don't-ever-fucking-go-there' side of town everywhere we went — special mentions include nearly side-swiping a car in Compton, getting stuck doing a 10-point turn as we woke up locals at midnight in New Orleans, and me being chased by a drug dealer with a knife through the back streets of Charleston, SC (don't ask)

- staying in a billionaire's mansion on a lake in Ontario, thanks to our well-connected Canadian buddy Blake

- seeing Ben Harper and Jack Johnson live at Jones Beach Theater on Long Island, NY.

We literally drove that poor car into the ground. For the last week or two smoke poured from the back as a waterfall of power-steering fluid leaked onto the muffler. Every time we filled up on gas we needed another bottle of fluid — another reflection on the Insufficient Funds life we were living!

Before setting off on this road trip, still in Canada and gaining some traction in our small community of newfound buddies, we printed a bunch more Insufficient Funds shirts, hoodies and caps and set off down the west coast. We funded some of the trip by selling our merch to randoms along the way. We'd strike up a conversation with almost anyone. They'd be drawn to us because of the accent, and we'd do deals out of the boot in all sorts of dodgy places.

We were going to be the next Hurley, who sold to Nike for $60 million. We'd cash in and never work a full-time job in our lives!

But … life got in the way. We went back to uni, finished our degrees, put on our sensible shirts and ties, and got our full-time jobs. At the time we didn't have the balls, maturity or foresight to really give it a crack.

The implications of 'Insufficient Funds' never lost traction though. In hindsight the philosophy of our little movement revolved around freedom, living day-to-day without a care in the world, having the means — just — to do everything we wanted. That was our life as 20-year-olds, the first wave of Millennials, and it was so relatable. Insufficient Funds offered a different, droll way of looking at that dismal $0 balance on the ATM slip.

# Our journey to Sufficient Funds

My name is James, and I have Sufficient Funds.

*Hold up, who is this wanker?*

Before you exercise that faved Aussie tradition of trimming the poppies, let me share a bit more of my story. With a British dad and an Aussie mum, I had an interesting and fortunate upbringing. Born in England, but moving to Australia when I was two years old, I spent most of my youth in and around Grafton in the Northern Rivers. My nanna lived 40 minutes up the Pacific Highway in the then sleepy coastal village of Yamba.

Grafton was an amazing place to grow up and I wouldn't have traded it for the world. In a country town, people's views on money are a bit different from those in the city, and the bar for financial success is set fairly low. I remember being labelled 'rich' by the boys at cricket one Saturday because Dad dropped me off in a late-model Ford Territory.

My parents were, and are still, comfortable but certainly not rich. They are a great example of people who spend money in line with their values. They're also proof that the idea of 'experiences not things' was around long before it was meme'd and made Instapopular. We were very lucky to have seen a good chunk of the world as kids, mostly on a shoestring, but we weren't rocking the new Nikes and I'm pretty sure I was in high school before I finally got my first pair of Quiksilver school shorts.

Some of these parental decisions were torture for me at the time, but looking back I came to see that without big incomes they did a cracking job of setting themselves up and giving my sister Kate and me a fantastic start. So from a young age I understood what Sufficient meant.

Fast forward a decade, with my university degree in hand, I ended up in finance. Initially I donned the suit and tie, sat in the corporate office looking over Sydney Harbour and embraced the wisdom of the suits who surrounded me. Over time, though, the pull of creating something more meaningful took over in me. The idea of focusing on what was truly Sufficient and being true to who I really was led me to ditch the suits and ties for boardies and T-shirts — and I never looked back.

Since then I've done a few more things to work towards both defining my version of Sufficient and achieving it. For the past two decades I have been working in the money world, helping individuals, couples and families with their money decisions and financial planning. Looking back on these years, I know I was absolutely destined to be where I am right now and I don't regret a thing. My wife Tash and I have built a business, Sufficient Funds, that serves people in a way that truly makes their world better. In turn,

Tash and I have created the freedom we've always dreamed of by running a super-lean operation that has been entirely virtual since way before COVID made it cool. We have an amazing team, with great systems, and as a family we now have complete freedom of location if we want it.

Talking about travel, we've also had a lot of fun along the way. I've travelled internationally on average at least once a year since a high-school exchange to Dachau, Germany, in 1999. I've surfed and snowboarded on four continents, made it to overseas weddings, thrown our own wedding, and visited friends and family wherever they happen to be in the world.

This is all part of our version of Sufficient Funds.

Could we have achieved many financial goals sooner?

Absolutely!

But it's never just about 'financial' goals for us, neither should it be for you.

You may be saying to yourself, 'That's all cool, James, but why is this book important to me?' Well, it wasn't all about making this work for us personally. As a professional, I've clocked over 10 000 hours of one-on-one with clients, helping them do this in their own lives.

This heavy devotion to repetition, improvement and feedback is what Todd Herman refers to in his book *The Alter Ego Effect* when talking about reaching a level of mastery in your field. This field for me is not just about providing financial advice, as my profession would define it, but in focusing on helping people make a successful connection between money and life and use it to truly live out their dreams.

I'll return to our journey to Sufficient Funds in later pages. Achieving, and reaching beyond, Sufficient Funds is exactly what you'll be doing if you read and implement the suggestions in this book.

## How this book works and why it's important to you

This book is not a guide to escaping from work. The idea of retirement as a life goal is flawed. It is based on the notion that you work in a job you don't love with people you can't stand and your sole aim is to get out the other end. Putting too much emphasis on retirement as the source of all happiness will likely leave you feeling short-changed when you discover it isn't the light at the end of the tunnel you dreamed about.

Achieving Sufficient Funds is not about retirement planning. It's something that can bear fruit much faster than that, and it's way more powerful.

It starts with acknowledging that you will always need some form of income to allow you to live.

Defining what is Sufficient for you is covered in chapter 1, and it all flows from there. You'll learn very quickly that the more you align your money decisions with the outcomes you want, the more clarity you'll gain over your future, the more confidence you'll have, the more momentum you'll build and, ultimately, the happier and more fulfilled you'll be!

Following the steps I outline will allow you to take action now towards living life on your own terms, spending money according to your values, and always having money for the experiences and things that seriously matter to you, now and forever!

I share a fair bit about me in these pages in the hope you can relate. This book gets far more personal than most (sorry to Tash, who puts up with my unabashed storytelling even though she is a much more private person). I share a lot about our lives here, as well as stories from people we've worked with, so you can see you're not alone in the challenges you face and that the solutions are very much within your reach.

With my training, hands-on experience, lust for adventure and no-holds-barred attitude to giving new things a crack, I've made that connection in my own life and we're now making it flow for our clients.

This book will give you the skills and strategies needed to implement your money plan in a way that allows you to live your ideal life. Once you've worked out your life plan, you need to implement your money plan. You also need to know how to reassess and adapt when the shit hits the fan.

There's plenty of information out there about the money side, but very little about how to make that much-needed connection to your life, which means you may struggle to implement your plan.

Experience has shown me that there are five important steps on the road from Insufficient to Sufficient Funds. These are:

1. Define

2. Declutter

3. Develop

4. Defend

5. Deliver.

To be very clear, I have found that only once you've nailed each of these five steps can you expect to achieve your goals, so I've structured the book accordingly and I strongly recommend that you read and action these stages in the order in which they are introduced.

In chapter 1: Define, I'll discuss the importance of mindset, and help you map out your particular definition of Sufficient Funds.

In chapter 2: Declutter, you'll learn how to set up a fail-safe system to remove money waste from your life, so every day you can smash out money moves like you've never done before.

Chapter 3: Develop is where the rubber really hits the road — think investments, tax and superannuation — but in a way that's easy to digest. This is where you move on from simply counting your chips to strategically building 'mad stacks' that link directly to the goals and values you defined in chapter 1.

By the end of chapter 4: Defend, you'll be fully equipped to shield yourself and your family from the inevitable bumps in the road. You'll discover how to bounce back after depleting your emergency buffer, strategies for sudden shifts, the interesting role of perspective and how to insure against the unforeseeable.

Finally, in chapter 5: Deliver, we bring it all home and discuss what comes next. If you have implemented everything in this book up to this chapter, you'll be well on your way to achieving Sufficient Funds. The trick now is to stay motivated and on track. Loaded with practical tips, and with a clear picture of how you can consistently redefine Sufficient, you will be unstoppable.

You've achieved Sufficient Funds, when you're clear and confident about your future, you have a protection plan and suitable buffers in place, and you're building mad stacks in all the areas you need to achieve all the big goals you've set for yourself.

I am seriously pumped about the results you'll get, but before we rip into it, a quick note about retirement.

# Fuck F.I.R.E.—why retirement is NOT the goal

You may have heard of the FIRE movement? Investopedia describes it as follows:

> *a movement dedicated to a program of extreme savings…By dedicating up to 70% of income to savings, followers of the FIRE movement may eventually be able to quit their jobs and live solely off small withdrawals from their portfolios decades before the conventional retirement age of 65.*

Firstly, to make FIRE work, you need to be one very 'special' human, someone who thrives on frugality, because you will spend years, even decades, spending next to nothing, saving like crazy, likely working a job you don't enjoy, to eventually quit and live off the pennies you've managed to squirrel away.

It might surprise you, but even as a financial guy, most extremely frugal people irk me. If you can live a low-cost life and be happy doing all the things you want to do, that's truly amazing. Good for you, but for the most part frugality is about extreme sacrifice. Spending nothing and as a result having no fun, is not a pathway I'm chasing. I've found too many fun things I love to do — think heli-skiing, mountain biking and regular travel — things that cost money and that I don't want to wait until I'm 65 to enjoy.

If you spend the best part of your work life saving a high percentage of your income, you'll actually find it difficult to unwind from this behaviour when you're finally able to stop and enjoy it. Look at Jack Welch, storied president of General Electric. He had a heart attack that nearly killed him at age 70. He said his biggest regret was how tight he'd been with his money. Growing up without much meant he squirrelled it all away. Even with his huge income and assets, he still wouldn't allow himself to stop and enjoy it, until it was almost too late. For your sake, I sincerely hope this isn't you, but if it is, this book will be insanely helpful in showing you how to achieve your version of Sufficient while allowing you to live *now*.

Another issue with FIRE is that you must rely heavily on consistent investment returns. The spreadsheet you downloaded from Mr Money Moustache's site — Google him, he's a bit of a hero, but not someone 99 per cent of us are likely to be able to emulate — is tracking your daily, weekly, monthly progress towards Financial Independence.

You're working your shitty, soul-sucking job, spending way too much time tweaking and updating your Excel file, sweating towards that day when you finally get to call it quits. Then an unexpected global event means the arse falls out of the share market, and 30 per cent is shaved off your investment balance in a matter of days. You're now working another five to 10 years to make this up. Soz…

We are living and breathing a very cool alternative, and so are our clients. Let's do this!

# CHAPTER ONE
# Define—the missing step

Define is your starting point on the road to Sufficient Funds. This is where you define, to the best of your ability right now, what a fulfilling and successful life looks like to you. As Nelson Mandela famously said, 'There is no passion to be found in settling for a life that is less than the one you are capable of living.'

My life's work has been bundled into the work we do every day in our aptly named business, Sufficient Funds. At its core, it's a financial planning and mortgage broking business. But, as you might have guessed, we spin things a little differently over here, and this is providing phenomenal results for the peeps we're working with.

One point of difference is our acceptance, as money nerds, that it's not all about money. In fact, when we first meet people, we put money aside completely and focus solely on 'Defining Sufficient'. This is motivating, fun and challenging. We focus on your life goals and values, so it forms the foundation for all your future money plans and decisions.

We park the money for this part because money is a repeat offender in creating limiting beliefs. When money is involved upfront it causes us to worry at the outset that we can't achieve our goals or won't ever be able to afford something we want. So right now please forget about the dollars, park your worries about debts and savings for a while. It's time to focus on your dreams.

# The power of positive thinking for financial wellbeing

Before we launch into defining your ideal life, I want to address the importance of having your mindset right.

I've never been criticised for not thinking big enough. I'm a dreamer. I've also never had a problem with convincing myself that whatever I want is achievable. According to CliftonStrengths, 'futuristic' and 'positivity' are among my top strengths. Someone once told me that I'm *too* positive. I'm not convinced that's possible as long as you channel it into action and back it up with an occasional dose of realism, though not too much of the latter.

In my experience, self-belief and positivity are the keys to getting started and jumping all the hurdles along the way.

When you have something massively meaningful to work towards you'll move mountains to make it happen. Even more so when you experience small wins and feed off the positivity of those wins when aiming towards your bigger goals. You're not only kicking goals, you're carving out your mindset.

Before we get stuck into your definition of Sufficient and how to get there, I want to share with you some achievements in my life where positive thinking and self-belief were required above all else.

I think back to my early days at university, planning for my exchange to Canada, where the seeds for this book first germinated. At the time, leaving behind all my friends and family for six months felt huge, but the excitement and enormity of what lay ahead made me save harder and put in the additional hours to organise myself and make it happen. The cost, the time to plan and prepare, and all the unknowns that scared me so much seemed like massive hurdles. But I passed all my classes, the trip happened, and I made friends and memories for life. Positive thinking and action turned those six months into a life-changing experience and one of the best and most memorable experiences I've ever had.

Fast forward to December 2006. Tash and I were recently engaged and on relatively low incomes. It was no Kim Kardashian rock, but I spent 80 per cent of two years' savings on the ring. For a 25-year-old in a low-level corporate position, I'd majorly splashed out. The bank balance was bleak and we had just over 12 months to save from scratch for a wedding and honeymoon, while also wanting to buy our first home. We were working our butts off to get ahead so we could make the life we wanted. Although we'd already travelled extensively both separately and together, we were determined to reward ourselves with a honeymoon that blew all our other trips out of the water.

Our challenge was to save 80 per cent of our combined after-tax income. After rent it left us with about $200/month to live on. This was a massive stretch for us, both financially and mentally. For the first time in our lives we were starting to earn decent money but we couldn't enjoy any of it.

## Understand that all life decisions have a money aspect to them.

This is one of those cases where money and life intersected in a big way, but more important than money was the positive thinking and self-belief needed to make it work. It required a focus on achieving our small goals and positively reinforcing that self-belief that we could get there.

As we saved hard for our wedding we also had to plan for it, book venues, send invites and book the honeymoon. We also started searching for our first home. I was negotiating simultaneously with real estate agents and cake decorators. I quickly learned the geography of Sydney as I visited clients who lived anywhere within 100 kilometres of where we lived, often arriving home very late at night. Tash was completing her Master's in Medical Science full time as well as climbing the ladder in her 10- to 12-hour-a-day job.

These challenges taught us to be organised, support each other, make the most of any spare time and not to sweat the small stuff. More importantly, it taught us self-belief and positivity. Without these key ingredients, all the planning, efficiency, saving and support in the world wouldn't have meant squat.

Everyone longs for Sufficient Funds, but few actually achieve it, mainly because they don't believe in themselves, and small obstacles turn into more couch time and less action.

We've had challenging times when mindset was just as crucial, including fertility and health challenges, stepping through surgeries and IVF, and helping our premmie newborn through major health challenges in the first few months of his life. Mindset, above all else, is what's left when everything else is depleted.

From these real-life experiences, here are my three super-basic but proven tips for framing your positive mindset for financial wellbeing:

1. **Avoid negativity.** You've heard this a thousand times. If they're not building you up, they're bringing you down. Remove the people in your life who bring you down or don't believe in you.

2. **Keep your head up (literally).** Okay, hear me out on this one. Without delving into any of the science behind this, stand tall as a giraffe and keep your posture like that of a soldier reporting for duty. Not only will it make you look like you're ready to take on the world, but it will also give you the mindset of a champion. Because when you stand tall and confident, you'll feel like you can conquer any challenge that comes your way, and achieve all the goals you've set for yourself.

3. **Create a series of small wins**. Celebrate your small financial victories and use these as fuel to propel yourself towards the bigger goals. We'll dive into your big goals shortly. When we get there you'll have a list. The first step is to break that list down into much smaller daily tasks. Do one thing every day to build momentum. Do this for a full fortnight and it will blow your mind how far you've come.

Self-belief and positive thinking will give you the combination of confidence and motivation you need to nail this chapter. Combine this with a desire to learn and grow, and you'll be unstoppable.

# How to spend a billion dollars: find your purpose and stay on it

Before you write down your big list you need to get clear on why you're on this Earth. Make sure you get the path right first, before you set off chasing the dollars.

There's a lot of content out there about finding your purpose in order to live successfully. Simon Sinek made it famous through the brilliant book *Start with Why*, and every guru out there now trumpets doing what you love as a top tip for success.

So now we're all fully aware that loving what you do means you'll be better at it, I want to share with you the fluff-free way to find your purpose and stay on track with it.

Start by getting crystal clear on your innate drivers. Take money off the table. In fact, take any constraint off the table and allow yourself to think about what you really want to do with the years you have on this Earth. Big-thinking billionaire Peter Diamandis says the way to find your purpose is by answering these two questions:

1. What did you really want to be when you were a kid? (This is what I mean by your innate drivers…)

2.  If someone gave you a billion dollars, how would you spend it and what would you do to improve the world? (…and this is removing the constraints.)

I believe the day you accept that you've become an adult and you need to get realistic about your future endeavours, dial back your dreams and live the life society has planned for you, is the day you die inside. A bit dramatic? No way!

Diamandis explains that thinking about what you wanted to be as a child and what you would do with a billion dollars can help you identify your passions and the things you care about. By exploring these questions, you gain insight into what drives you and what kind of impact you want to make on the world. He is relating this to the business world, and specifically to what kind of company you might start to solve a big-world problem, but we can apply this equally at a personal level for our own achievements in our own lives.

The real kicker is question number 2. Pause on this for a second. A billion dollars is more than you could spend on all the things you've ever dreamed of. It's more than you'd need for the house, jet, yacht, all the travel, cars, and to never work again. You can have all of this if you want it, but popping bottles and dropping thousands on blackjack and private jets will get boring real quick, and you'll still have millions in the bank.

## ACTIVITY
## Find your purpose

Stop here and think about these two questions. Ultimately, when money is no longer an issue, how will you keep yourself

(continued)

interested, motivated, alive? Block some time in your calendar, free yourself from all distractions, even go off grid to get clear, then dive in and answer these questions. Some people find this comes straight to them; others will need to do a massive brain dump first. If that's you, grab a pen and paper and let the stream of consciousness flow.

Grasp that childhood dream or whatever is burning you up inside and channel it. This is the fuel that will have you jumping all the hurdles to create the life you want to live. Cast back to when life and your dreams were completely free of money constraints.

Once you have your list, tidy it up and put it somewhere so you can refer to it often. When we work through Defining Sufficient with our clients we like to add images that relate to their goals—if you're a visual person absolutely do this and create yourself a vision board that will help you stay on purpose.

Next, learn to live your life with an undying focus on this.

Once you find your purpose, the hard part is keeping it always front of mind. Here are my tips for remaining on track:

# 1. Control your social media addiction

'Social media is like crack,' says Gary Vaynerchuk, '— immediately gratifying and hugely addictive.' I admit, social media has taken a lot of my time. It's a bit of a catch-22 for me, as I need it for business and I enjoy it. We use it to build a community around what we're doing at Sufficient Funds, elevating our brand, sharing our clients' stories and reaching more people.

I also waste a lot of time on it.

These platforms are built to pull you in and keep you there. Understand that when you take your phone to the loo, or just have that quick squiz at Insta to see if you've got any more likes on your baby spam (guilty!), you lose more than just that short amount of time. You lose your train of thought on the work you were doing and drain some of the remaining focus you have for the day, making it far more difficult to get back to the big stuff.

## 2. Say it out loud

Public accountability with the right people is hugely valuable.

Ever signed up for a fun run, told everyone you're doing it, then had to pull out? If you're anything like me, you'd bend over backwards to make sure you keep your word. Same goes for big goals. Tell your friends, tell your family, tell your neighbours. Go ahead and tell the barista at your local cafe. The last thing you need is to have to change up your local coffee spot because you've made exactly zero progress towards your goals. The more you say it out loud, the more likely you are to follow through.

A word of warning: if you have a big crazy idea, don't let it out of the bag too early. Most people won't yet be on your wavelength. Trying to paint the vision of something that doesn't exist yet to the wrong people (who are probably your nearest and dearest) is a fast way to having it shut down before you get started. You need at least a few success points and a sense that it's going to work to get you past the naysayers when they hear about your secret mission.

# 3. Learn to say no

If you're anything like me you'll see an opportunity to help, a new business idea or something that seems like a lot of fun, everywhere you look. You'll find it incredibly challenging to have eight careers or start multiple businesses all at once.

I've had to train myself to avoid shiny object syndrome by pausing and holding the mirror up to see if it aligns with my values. Saying no to anything that doesn't align is imperative.

Remember that when you find your purpose, you're working towards the most fulfilling life you could possibly live. Anything that draws you away from this needs to be treated with the kind of disdain you'd direct at a used bandaid in a public pool.

# 4. Don't compare

When you find your purpose, you gain the opportunity to live a life true to that purpose. Nothing in the world is more valuable and fulfilling than this.

We'll dive into this in chapter 2, but be careful not to look next door to see what your neighbour's life looks like. They don't have your skills, your ideals or your purpose. What ultimately makes them tick won't be the same as what does it for you. Do yourself a favour and leave them out of it!

## ACTIVITY
## Start your Defining Sufficient list

Create a list of everything that's coming up for you, and build this into your grand list of goals and values for the foreseeable future.

My hot tip: keep it old school and use a pen and paper. It's crucial to have a physical copy that you can pin on a note board or stick on the wall somewhere you're going to see it regularly.

Add to this list as you read and work through the rest of this chapter.

Note that this list is never set in concrete. It will need to remain flexible as you grow and life happens, but starting now is crucial.

Note for couples: you will have individual goals as well as joint and perhaps family goals. If you're a couple who are planning a life together I strongly recommend you join forces on this list. But first spend 20 minutes individually making your list and then use the time together to discuss it all. This is an important step to ensure that each of you retains your individuality but that you also have a chance to discuss upfront where your views and values differ. This is an important step for jointly working towards achieving Sufficient Funds.

# Three steps to setting bigger adventures (and how we get there with our clients)

Constantly striving for bigger adventures is what makes me tick, and helping others achieve this for themselves is why I do what I do

11

for a living. Here I want to give you some insider tips on how to do this in three key steps.

When we kick off one of our Defining Sufficient sessions, I ask open-ended questions about what you're striving towards, with the goal of understanding what makes you tick. It's also a great way to gauge how you feel about your current situation, as well as how confident you are about your future and your ability to achieve the targets you've set yourself.

These are not always easy questions to answer and over the years I've noticed a strong recurring theme: we are uneasy talking about our big ideas and far more comfortable listing the usual goals society tells us we *should* strive for.

It starts with what you think I want to hear, which is usually one of these four bad boys:

- Pay off debt.

- Save more.

- Reduce tax.

- Start investing.

Through no fault of your own, and mainly because our profession has created this perception, this is the default position of almost every new client. 'He's a financial adviser, so I'd better tell him something financial.'

Often people start with the goal of buying a property. This is a great goal to have if it really matters to you, but so often clients can't tell me why they want to do this. 'Well, everyone does it, so shouldn't we?'

There's that word: *should.*

Next comes the lesser material things: a new car, wardrobe, kitchen, fence, coffee table...

These can be really important, and even impact your quality of life. Typically you notice the things that are closest to you first. They are okay as immediate needs and often take some deliberate saving to acquire. Note that ticking some of these items off the list can also help remove a few distractions and give you greater clarity on the mindset you need to tick off the big things, but do it understanding the impact of this on your overall financial situation, and again ensure you are truly going to value it.

We've now made a shopping list of the relatively small items that have been hanging around for some time. They're a very valid part of the conversation but we're far from the gold at this point.

I mentioned my parents' philosophy of 'buying experiences, not things'. Well, this meme has been overshared for a reason. Material acquisitions don't necessarily make us happy. They usually fulfil a short-term need and are quickly devalued, to be thrown out or replaced down the track.

We're usually about 25 minutes into the meeting by this point, and this is where the discussion typically falters. I've got the financial stuff and your latest shopping list, but what comes next often takes some serious prompting.

This is where the magic happens. Some would challenge the idea that true goal-setting is beyond the realm of financial advice but I call total BS on this. Once you're clear on your purpose and you've put all thoughts of the dollars aside, you start to remember all of the things that are important to you. If you don't do this first, any money plans will eventually fall over, or will not lead you to where you really want to be.

To help you think past your immediate shopping list, I want to show you what I'd typically suggest to clients when the time is right.

Here are my three steps to helping you achieve bigger adventures and get more out of life.

## Step 1: Deal with 'you'

It can be uncomfortable imagining ourselves in a better position. Over time the inevitable hurdles of life can chip away at our confidence and ability to dream.

The good news is that this is temporary and reversible.

Make a short list of what you would call your strengths and weaknesses; aim for three of each. Start with strengths, as these are usually easier to bring to the surface. With weaknesses, think about recent times you've failed to achieve something. Maybe you thought about starting a business but didn't get it off the ground, or you failed to reach a weight-loss goal or a savings target for a holiday and you're still paying off the credit card. What is it about you that made these goals difficult? You don't need to fix these areas in your life but you need to be aware of them and to be honest with yourself so you can work around it when the time comes.

This might make you uncomfortable, but if you don't know yourself well enough the next two steps will be fruitless. Take out your phone or a pen and get started! If you get stuck, ask someone close to you, your partner or a good friend, to help out.

I used the CliftonStrengths Top 5 Talent Assessment to find my strengths. This test is used by the biggest companies in the world to help their staff understand their talents and maximise their potential. It's not expensive and is well worth doing when you consider the positive impact. You'll wind up with a ranked list of your top five strengths and plenty of detail on what it all means. You can pay a bit more and get a full list of 34.

Far better to amplify your strengths than to get too caught up in your weaknesses. Be aware of them, certainly; create strategies to work around these weaknesses, work to complement your skills and move on. You'll already know your shortcomings, and rubbing it in isn't overly helpful. Put your strengths in the spotlight and go for it!

Every time I see my list of strengths, they strike a chord. I know they're 100 per cent accurate, which also confirms why I love the work I do.

You'll find they're relevant not only in your career or business, but in everything you do. The process will give you massive confidence when it comes to learning more about yourself and preparing you for the next steps in this book. Remember, a key element of achieving

Sufficient Funds isn't stopping work forever, but enjoying the work you do so you don't feel the need to escape it.

## Step 2: Think bigger

Now you have at least some of your key strengths down on paper and you've thought about the weaknesses you want to avoid, it's time to leave the small things behind. Clear the runway, it's time to chase down your biggest ever hopes and dreams.

In his old-school but still relevant book *The Magic of Thinking Big*, David Schwartz suggests, 'Look at things not as they are, but as they can be. Visualization adds value to everything. A big thinker always visualizes what can be done in the future.'

This could be anything. I'm not going to tell you what to aim for, but when you're thinking about this stuff, it has to get the heart pumping. Make sure it excites you. I might not roll out of bed for a wet weekend caravanning in Tamworth, but I'd consider trading my first-born for a week heli-skiing in the Canadian Rockies.

Your goals need to be big enough to give you the motivation to chase them down. A good yardstick for this is, when you tell your family about it, expect to get answers such as, 'Why would you want to do that?' or 'That sounds hard' or 'That's too dangerous — you're not a risk taker' or 'How could you afford to do that?'

To prime your thinking, here are some examples I've loved hearing from my clients:

- Buy a yacht and sail the world for 12 months.

- Rent an apartment in Barcelona for three months, become fluent in Spanish and enjoy long weekends in Paris and the Swiss Alps.

- Take a family road trip around America in a Winnebago.

- Take a career break to test out my dream of becoming a chef.

- Build a side-hustle online based on my passion for collecting Lego.

When you start to think bigger, you become wired that way. You train your brain to challenge society's norms and become a free spirit, an individual (or couple or family) on a mission to smash your goals.

Don't forget to write these down too. If it's not written down, it won't happen!

## Step 3: Take action NOW

Take one of your big dreams and break it down. What is the one thing you can do right now to move this forward? Do a five-minute web search for second-hand yachts and get some quotes. Subscribe to various airline sites to get across their upcoming sales or use a Google flight hack (Google it!). Or find a blog about someone else who has already done what you want to do, and reach out for advice.

For all the list makers out there, ask ChatGPT to make the list for you. Feed it the goal (with all the specifics you already know) and ask it to provide you with a detailed 10-step list of how to get started. You might need to tweak it slightly for you, but it's a great place to start.

Do one thing each day for three days in a row, then watch the magic happen. Momentum will build and before you know it you'll be on track to become the world's first family to climb Mount Everest in matching onesies!

'The path to success is to take massive, determined action.' Who doesn't love a good Tony Robbins quote? But don't just think about it — it's time to act.

## ACTIVITY
## Three steps to bigger adventures

Stop now and take 30 minutes to work through the following three steps:

1. Make a list of your strengths and weaknesses.

2. Write down one big goal that really sets your heart pumping.

3. Take one small action right now to move you towards this goal. Once done, set your intention for the next small actions that you'll complete tomorrow and the next day. Continue this for a full fortnight and you'll be well on your way!

Add this new big goal to the Defining Sufficient list you started in the previous activity.

# Experiences or things—why can't I have both?

We've touched on this already, and it's guaranteed to pop up as a recurring theme as you continue to define your Sufficient life. 'Buy experiences not things' is a popular meme for good reason. Choosing materialism (more possessions) over experiencing what the world has to offer is a terrible waste. Minimalism is trending and no one wants to be the hoarder on the block.

Most people tend to naturally favour one over the other, and many couples I work with are learning the art of compromise to allow for both in their lives. Of course, experiences and things are not mutually exclusive, and sometimes you need to just chill out and run with whatever gets you going at that point in time.

One thing I'll never do is tell you there is only one way to live your life. What tickles you in all the right places is none of my business. I can provide all the guidance in the world and ask challenging questions to help you get there, but in the end it's all about you.

The best financial advisers and life coaches I know always remain impartial. When it comes to experiences and/or things, you do you. Following this process, either solo or with a partner, will demand that you consider where your values lie. Just remember that wherever you end up is fine.

Knowing this will help you navigate the twists and turns on the road to Sufficient Funds and accelerate towards your goals with confidence.

## The case for experiences

It's hard to hide my bias here. We are well and truly sold on the case for experiences, and I'm sure many of you are as well. Experiences are number one for me. They're the stuff my dreams are made of.

My objectives are heavily oriented towards experience, and they are broad. From trying something new on the weekend and mixing up our family activities, to as much global travel as we can get, we find our eyes are opened by experiencing all that comes with a new destination, seeing different ways of life and points of view.

Experiences don't have to relate to travel. They could involve learning a new skill, like cooking or a foreign language, trying your hand at painting or photography, or spending six months building towards a fitness goal, like competing in a triathlon.

Note some of the above involve the purchase of things, but these purchases are a means to an end, rather than the goal itself.

The rise of the sharing economy allows the more hardcore on this side of the fence, which we are not, to forgo owning a house, car, bike or boat, instead directing all funds to real-life moments. These are interesting times we live in.

## The case for things

Friends of ours recently purchased an obscenely expensive sound system for their house. They have other goals, a mortgage and a love for travel, but being musos and spending a lot of time at home, a high-quality sound system was just the thing to enhance their lifestyle.

The message here: don't let the meme screw with your reality.

Our family spends 75 per cent of our lives eating, sleeping, living and working in the 'thing' that Tash and I saved to purchase together. We've upgraded our home twice since that first purchase and we wouldn't have it any other way. Don't hesitate to allocate funds towards things that enhance your quality of life. The only caveat: make sure there's a purpose, a clear benefit, and that it fits with everything else you want to achieve.

For many, working towards their goals accounts for a big chunk of their time. If, like us, you have bigger targets for yourself, chances are you'll do better if home is a place of comfort where you can wind down and enjoy all the things that make you happy. There's nothing wrong with that.

Spending funds on material things that enhance your life experience — the home itself, car, backyard office/granny flat for working from home, an infrared sauna, a serious mattress to ensure quality shuteye — these are totally cool. As I said, if it makes your life more Sufficient, go nuts.

For the most part, experiences and things go together. Give yourself permission to run with or against the herd, or dangle your legs either side of the fence for a while. Just make sure you're doing it for you and no one else.

# It's not meant to be easy—be prepared to work

Sometimes I think back to our story of selling Insufficient Funds T-shirts and dreaming of it becoming our multimillion-dollar baby. It was all about the fairy tale of what success looked like.

I was in Yamba with family sometime after the big US road trip. The founder of Billabong had recently built a mansion up the road in Angourie. I imagined his life of surfing, partying and travelling the world with mates, not the work he did and continued to do to get there. The idea of selling T-shirts to create the world we wanted to live gave me chicken skin (yep, that's the emotional side that helps me dream big).

What I've learned since 2004, though, is that action beats everything, and dreams alone won't get you far. In fact, they'll cloud your judgement if you let them take over. It took me a long time to figure this out.

In my early career I spent several years grinding it out and learning the ropes. I realised very early on that there was a big difference between those who made it to a management role and those who settled in the trenches and were destined for minimal pay rises for the rest of their lives.

Simon Sinek hadn't yet given his famous TED talk, YouTube and life-hacking hadn't arrived, so we were stuck with 'work hard, learn lots, get promoted, earn more'.

I was straight out of uni and there were people in their 40s being managed by those in their 20s.

I knew where I needed to be.

## Set lofty goals and maintain a strong work ethic

Tash and I had set ourselves some fairly lofty income goals when we first moved in together in 2005, including six-figure salaries by 30. It became a bit of a competition. I now see this with clients all the time. Starting out on $35k each after uni, 3 per cent p.a. wasn't going to cut it.

Tash completed her Master's while working full time. I was driving up to 100 km from the office to meet clients, sometimes getting home well after midnight, before starting back in the CBD at 7.30 am the next day.

We started climbing the ladder and both of us achieved our income goal by age 27. We didn't set out with an intentional work ethic, but looking back, our work ethic was a key factor in getting us there.

## Work smarter AND harder

These days, as I build my financial services businesses, I'm looking for all the shortcuts available to streamline processes and become more efficient.

As advisers, our strength is in talking to clients, building relationships with them so they have the confidence to share their dreams and we can then work together with them on their biggest money decisions. This is what we enjoy, and we're very good at it.

It's easy to get bogged down in all the paperwork that is inherent in this type of work. I've learned that the best way to avoid this is by practising pseudo-laziness: 'How can I remove myself from this to make it better.'

If my strength is in working directly with my clients, coaching my team and promoting the amazing work we're doing, I need to look at everything else as a complete waste of my time. This is why our clients don't just get to know me, or our other financial advisers; they get to know our team members. There are obviously many benefits to us and our clients because of this, none more so than my not getting bogged down in the tasks that are not in my list of strengths, allowing me to focus on the value-adding conversations and Money Action Plans (MAP)™ that we're privileged to be delivering.

Here are my tips for being smarter when it comes to tackling tasks on the way to achieving Sufficient Funds:

- **Leverage technology.** Good tech is cheap — often free — and allows us to automate repetitive tasks. Just as you will learn to do with your money in the next chapter, automation helps you free your time for more impactful or creative work.

- **Prioritise.** Not all tasks are created equal. It's good to have a to-do list but ensure that it's leading you to the big outcomes you're seeking to achieve. Then, crucially, break the tasks into 15- to 20-minute items and work on only one thing at a time.

- **Embrace 'no'.** Learning to decline requests that don't align with my biggest goals or with my values remains an ongoing challenge for me. I'm partial to bright, shiny objects, but I've pushed myself to be better in this area and protect my calendar as ultimately it's the only way to progress as quickly as you'll need to when setting meaningful and significant goals.

- **Plan your downtime.** This is my favourite. When on a mission, whether it's building a business or striving for other massive milestones in your life, you need to have regular breaks to ensure you stay fresh and energised. You know that feeling you get at the start of January, ready to tackle a new year? Well, regular breaks throughout the year will help you rinse and repeat so you'll never simply flop into Christmas again.

As you hack your way to freedom, don't forget that this isn't about becoming idle; it's about creating time and the headspace to double down on your strengths.

Combining this with hard work will mean you leapfrog those who haven't figured this out yet, or are too stuck in their ways to act on it, and move swiftly towards the outcomes you seek.

## Push the boundaries

Walt Disney said, 'If you can dream it, you can do it.' Don't settle. Don't assume what you were capable of achieving last year is all you will be able to achieve in the year ahead. Be prepared to take risks and get comfortable being uncomfortable.

Forget everyone else, be the tall poppy — this is about *your* personal growth. These ideas are relevant to business owners and employees alike. If you don't embrace the importance of having a strong work ethic early, you'll miss all of the upside of being young and the opportunity to set yourself up for Sufficient Funds sooner.

This is your time to take risks and push the boundaries of what you think you're capable of, but none of it will pay off without periods of consistent hard work and long hours in pursuit of your dreams. Get stuck in.

## Buying happiness in Kuwait, and why you need challenge in your life

One time at a conference I had the pleasure of hearing a keynote from peak performance researcher Adam Fraser.

During his talk Dr Fraser spoke about how he was hired by the Kuwaiti government to help make the country happier. The talk had a number of focus points but this one stuck out, so I did some digging.

It turns out that Kuwait has had an amazing history of resilience and innovation. At the same time, they have amassed great wealth from their three main industries, banking, telco and of course oil.

It's well understood that in recent times their solution to almost every problem has been to throw cash at it, the prime focus being keeping the Kuwaiti nationals happy. Citizens enjoy many benefits (not available to foreign nationals), including interest-free housing loans, free education and healthcare, and low-cost land. In 2011 they were given free food for 13 months!

This all sounds pretty good, right?

Wrong. As Dr Fraser explained, one result of their extreme privilege was a deep sense of entitlement. He recounted how it's not unusual to see families hanging out at the beach on a mid-week afternoon instead of working, and to see 18-year-olds cruising around in Rolls-Royces and Bentleys. They are given or can purchase whatever they need or want yet despite this overall happiness levels have declined. It turns out that removing life's challenges, imagining this would make everyone happier, has in fact had the opposite effect.

There are some key lessons we can all take away from this on the road to Sufficient Funds.

## BEING TOO COMFORTABLE MAY HAVE A NEGATIVE IMPACT

If you're left not wanting for anything, you are unlikely to try very hard. It is for this reason that wealthy parents need to teach their kids how to grow their own wealth and make their own way in the world, regardless of what they may be set to inherit.

## HAVING A CHALLENGING GOAL TO STRIVE TOWARDS IS KEY TO REMAINING MOTIVATED

This is why I've highlighted the need to think big when setting your goals. Set them at a level that will really push you. If you're not motivated, you're unlikely to jump any hurdles as they arise.

## YOUR SENSE OF SELF-WORTH DEPENDS ON OVERCOMING CHALLENGES

Toddlers are great for highlighting this. Their rate of growth is exponential. We watch them learn to crawl, walk, talk, feed themselves, swim, ride a bike and countless other new tricks, it's crazy to see them gain the confidence they need and move on to the next thing.

Our kids as toddlers had bumps and bruises all over as they were constantly falling over, colliding with the furniture and throwing things at each other. This is really tough but we've always tried not to be 'helicopter parents' in the hope of building their resilience. Even before they hit three years old we were seeing massive confidence building as a result. Sure, they fall down and cry every now and then, but a few scratches are only going to strengthen them for the years to come. It's kind of cool to see this playing out as they grow, especially in their willingness to try new things and not shy away from challenges. As Tony Robbins puts it, 'progress equals happiness'.

This is true for adults too, but as we 'settle down' (urgh!), our growth can be much slower and we're more likely to become set in our ways.

This is why so many people who win the lotto end up struggling. They skipped all the hurdles that are part of accumulating financial assets.

The Kuwait example shows us how unhappy we could become if we were to rely on someone else to dictate our future. If you think someone else will do it for you, or that is your plan, it will likely end in tears.

The major lesson here: you create your own future. Use this chapter to do exactly that.

# Sufficiently Defined

In this chapter:

■ You've set your positive mindset for financial wellbeing, including setting your series of small wins to build momentum around good financial decisions. Do one thing every day for a full fortnight.

■ You've started and built on your very own Defining Sufficient list! Remember it's a moving beast, so keep it close and keep building on it.

■ You've weighed up what you'd do if you were totally financially free and asked yourself how those dreams fit with your purpose in life.

■ You've identified one big adventure or goal you're planning to tackle first, and you have set this in motion by ticking off the first few simple steps to make it happen.

■ You've taken time out from your day-to-day to define what a fulfilling and successful life looks like to you, and you have a clear list of what goals will make up your Sufficient life.

You've now worked through some important steps that so many unwittingly skip on their financial planning journey. This is where I see so many fail and why our clients, who always start here, get off to a flying start!

Massive congrats! You now have a solid understanding of your definition of Sufficient Funds. Keep this front of mind as we step through the next steps of decluttering your finances.

# CHAPTER TWO
# Declutter— clearing the path

Once you've Defined Sufficient and got clear on why you're doing all this, it's time for the hard yards, or the not-so-hard-now-you-know-where-to-start yards.

This chapter is all about creating the simplicity and space to do your best work. To make your money work. To make your money flow.

One thing I'm absolutely not going to do here is give you another one-size-fits-all budgeting tool or approach that you've seen in every book you've ever read on the subject. Even if you feel your current savings/spending system is working, I promise you'll get a lot out of this chapter. After all, you've just got super clear on your biggest goals and values. Now it's time to realign your current systems with this and remove any excess that may be lying around. It's time to Marie Kondo your money!

This is no joke. Most of our inability to take action in life is due to our being disorganised and unintentionally allowing a bunch of crap to get in the way right when we're ready to leap. Life's much better when our finances are fully decluttered.

In this chapter we'll first explore the critical importance of having a clear mindset, then you'll get super practical with some easy-to-follow steps to gain a better understanding of your financial position and ensure it all flows. Follow these steps and you'll be well on your way to achieving financial clarity and taking control of your money.

# Clarity: attitude and focus

It's widely reported that money is the biggest source of stress in the world. The American Psychological Association (APA), and the Australian Psychological Society (APS), which produces the annual National Stress and Wellbeing in Australia Survey, report that personal finances and concern around rising costs of everyday items is leading to significant stress and more serious health issues. The APA reports that money concerns were even higher than concerns around global uncertainty in 2022, despite its being a year full of pandemic stress and nuclear threats.

If you're constantly stressed about money, you'll find it difficult to be motivated and positive about your future, and without this motivation you won't get far. To reach Sufficient Funds and beyond, you need clarity and confidence. After many years of working with clients to create this, I've seen the magic that ensues once you get it right, and I want to share this with you.

Clarity gives you confidence, which builds momentum and puts you in your flow state, where you are untouchable. We want you to create a system for your money that will free you from distraction, one

32

that ensures you can navigate difficult times, changes in markets and family emergencies seamlessly. In turn, it will help you build towards the good times that you're striving for: more free time, the opportunity to explore the world, do meaningful and fulfilling work, start a family, help those in need…

This money system is free of clutter, because it remains focused solely on what it needs to do, so your money plan starts to facilitate the life you want to live. The core of your system is what we call Cruise Control: Your Spending Plan.

We'll get to this shortly, but first it's important to get your head in the game.

## Attitude: when it comes to income, it's not size that matters

There's a big difference between earning lots and having lots. I've been self-employed since 2015. I resigned from my well-paid corporate gig right after we bought our dream home and took out a mortgage that really stretched us. I then started a business with no clients. Looking back on it, we didn't have a fucking clue what we were doing at the start, but we survived.

I think a lot in terms of business, but the truth of the matter is that a business and your personal money flow aren't all that different.

Even though revenue (think total sales or total income) is often a measure of success for a business, it's a false measure as it tells only part of the story. A better yardstick is profit, or even better, cashflow. You can generate lots of income but if you aren't charging appropriately or you have a bloated staff base or other cost inefficiencies, there'll be little to no profit left and your business will run out of cash.

Think about your personal money life in the same way. Your salary is your revenue. Your profit is the money left over after all your spending. Success isn't in your $50k, $150k or $300k salary. This is only part of the equation. Many of the people I work with earn half as much as the big earner and still save more.

There's a tunnel vision that takes over when life revolves around 'make money, spend money', and there's not much light at the end of it. But once you're in the tunnel, it can be hard to find the exit. It's addictive. Why? Because the act of spending itself becomes the 'reward'. So you put in the hard yards just for the joy of spending the big bucks, not necessarily for what you are left with at the end of the day.

When Tash and I were in our late 20s we were working long, stressful hours but the money was good. Those Insufficient Funds ATM slips were a distant memory and we'd made the shift from our uni days when it was all time and no money to the polar opposite.

After funding the wedding we made a great start by purchasing our first home and an investment property within 18 months, but we didn't have the mental capacity or, more important, the systems in place to make good financial decisions.

We did a fair bit of what I would call binge spending. There were expensive overseas trips, business-class flights, luxury resort stays, and lots of eating out and takeaways. With no time to think, we made money decisions on the fly, with little or no consequences if we overspent as we could rely on being paid again next fortnight.

Some would think we had it made, we were walking on air, but in truth we look back on those times and think, geez we're glad we woke up when we did. We had to shift our mindset from head in the sand, spend every dollar to really understanding what we valued and consciously not allowing ourselves to 'waste' any excess.

Shifting this mindset changed our world. Being aware of the money coming in and money going out sounds like a simple concept, but it's less so when you remove time and consequence from the equation. As in an episode of *Hoarders*, it's scarily easy to create such a mess that you truly have no idea what lies beneath the surface.

Working hard, earning lots and having an abundance of financial resources is a great objective, and will let you do some pretty cool shit, but this only works when linked to your definition of Sufficient and when your spending aligns with this.

On the flipside, if you're already truly enjoying the work you do, then you should recognise that the grass is usually not greener on the other side. You may not be earning all the money in the world, but that's okay. You have something that a lot of people can only ever dream of. Stop and reflect on this. It's worth a lot more than you might think.

## Focus

I meditate most days, and have done for the past few years, often using the Headspace app. This app is split into a bunch of different sections based on what you're trying to deal with at the time (confidence, stress, appreciation, anxiety, balance and so on). One I find myself frequently returning to is called 'Finding Focus'. In this part, the instructor, Andy, talks about the idea of innate focus always being with us. My take on this is that instead of having to create this for yourself and then struggle to ensure you don't lose it again, you can have the confidence to accept that it's always there for you to tap into. As Andy says, it's kind of like knowing that the blue sky is always there and although it can become hidden or distorted by clouds, if you always remember it's there, then you instantly feel better and it's easier to manage distractions.

This concept can be readily applied to decluttering your finances. If the definition of declutter is to remove unnecessary items from an untidy or overcrowded place, it can equally apply to your overcrowded mind when you need to focus: right now that overcrowded place is where you are making your day-to-day money decisions. Think about your bank accounts, credit cards and any debts. By simplifying your money and decluttering you free up more headspace and reduce stress.

A sustained focus is key to remaining on track. Understand that you have an innate ability to focus with clarity on your money decisions. You just need the time, space and willpower to do it.

To be clear, by decluttering I'm not saying you need to remove money from your world. Quite the opposite. You need a system that ensures that every cent you earn flows into the right place with as little effort as possible.

Decluttering every aspect of your life allows you to be more productive and creative. You waste less time, spend more time on things that are meaningful for you and feel healthier.

Now let's get practical!

# Build your financial launchpad

Let's put the LeBaron in the garage for a hot minute — it's time to talk rockets.

When building a house you don't start with all the fancy bits. As nice as it might sound, all the good stuff, like putting the pool in, dropping the free-standing bath into the new ensuite, or kicking back with a Corona by the fire pit and sliding freshly kneaded dough into the outdoor pizza oven, doesn't come first. These are the cherries on top once all the work has been done.

Basics first. It's time to build your financial launchpad!

For most of us, school didn't teach us a single thing about money and sadly, for the same reason I'm writing this book, a lot of parents aren't equipped to teach their kids either.

The money stuff tends to get messy quickly. It's not uncommon for us to see a 25-year-old with a bit of personal debt here, some savings over there, a micro-investing account, some random shares, and of course plans to buy property. In fact, it's quite rare to meet someone who hasn't gone straight for the pizza oven, before laying the bricks and putting the roof on.

*A side note:* You're never too old to get this part right, so even if you're 55 and don't have it all sorted and working for you yet, do not skip this!

Your launchpad is your starting point, your clear runway. It's the foundations of your money house that support everything else you're going to do. A robust launchpad will also help you accelerate anything else you build on top.

Here are the three components of your launchpad:

1. **Dealing with debt.** Start with a new rule: *no personal debt*. This includes credit card and lifestyle debt; some loans (such as for car and house) are okay.

2. **Cruise Control: Your Spending Plan.** We've been using this system personally and with our clients for many years now. Done right, it will put your basic money sitch on steroids and help you keep more of what you earn and make far more confident day-to-day money decisions. This one is a game changer.

3. **Protection plan.** WTF is this? It's life insurance and income protection. Chapter 4 covers this in more detail, but I'm dripping this one in slowly to save you from closing the book, skipping away and burying your head in the sand.

Once you have these sorted you can then run out and tackle all the big things. Go nuts!

I'm keeping this light but it will give you the tools and a few ideas on how to get there more quickly.

# Dealing with debt

Let's face it, personal debt can be overwhelmingly stressful. I'm referring here to what is loosely known as 'bad debt'. Whether it's credit cards, personal loans or both, the feeling of owing money can leave us feeling trapped and anxious. The good news is there are steps you can take to get back in control of your finances and start feeling confident again.

In this chapter we explore some practical tips and strategies that can help you tackle your debt and keep rolling towards Sufficient Funds!

## The good ol' snowball vs avalanche

There are two commonly known methods for smashing multiple debts such as credit cards and personal loans. The *debt avalanche* involves making minimum payments on all debt, then using any remaining money to pay off the debt with the highest interest rate. The *debt snowball* involves paying off the smallest debts first to get them out of the way before moving on to the bigger ones (see figure 2.1).

The best method for you depends on whether you're driven by behaviour and reward (snowball) or pure financial benefit (avalanche). Chances are it's the former. You'll save more interest with the avalanche but this doesn't help if you feel like you're getting nowhere chipping away at what might also be the biggest debt and therefore the slowest to kill.

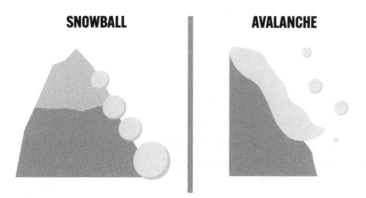

**SNOWBALL**          **AVALANCHE**

**Figure 2.1: Smashing debt: snowball vs avalanche**

The snowball will work better if you're an achiever who likes to tick off milestones. Hitting the smallest debt first will remove it from your life, and you'll have fewer payments to worry about moving forward.

If I had to lean in one direction, I'd opt for the snowball as most money issues stem from behaviour and, fundamentally, just staring at the numbers and relying on this only works for a select few of us (definitely not me!).

# Debt disruption strategies: creative ways to pay off debt

If you've taken the approach with your bank accounts that so long as you don't log in all will be fine, make today the day you lift up the bonnet and take a look. Ignorance is not bliss when it comes to your money, or lack thereof. I've seen this all too often. You're far better off dealing with it now, so read on. I'm confident this chapter will provide you with the rocket fuel to smash any debts. No more boring debt reduction plans. Time to get creative and, I dare say, even enjoy the process of smashing those bills!

There are plenty of traditional methods and advice for paying off debt, most of which have some value. You've heard them all before: create a budget, spend less than you earn, cut up that inessential credit card, earn more, make higher repayments, set up forced savings, pay the highest interest rate first, automate your repayments, consolidate your debts...

I've spent more than a decade helping people with these types of strategies, and with the right mindset and consistency they do work, but none of them are very exciting or creative. Often the best strategy for paying off debt is to keep it interesting, to shake things up. I want to show you some ways to make this happen.

This is by no means an all-encompassing list, but here's some less conventional, sometimes even controversial ways to get you thinking more creatively about paying off debt and freeing yourself from this mess.

## Find some quick wins

Quick wins give you a feeling of accomplishment and this positive reinforcement helps you to develop positive habits. They keep you motivated to continue along your path and push through difficult barriers.

Develop a habit with a series of quick wins. This will help you build the foundations of staying on top of your finances and make it seem effortless.

## Foil the fraudsters

This is huge yet most of the peeps aren't doing it. Check all your credit and debit card statements for bank or merchant errors as well as fraud. I usually do this about once a month. I go back through every item and make sure I know what it was. I've wrongfully (generously?) paid for all sorts of things on my credit card, from a women-only gym membership in Brisbane to a Chinese restaurant in Mexico City and, most recently, someone else's phone bill. It's happened to me at least 10 times over the past few years, and this checking exercise alone has helped me claw back more than $4000.

## Quick search for double-ups

List your regular payments. Okay, I threw in one really boring one for good measure. I suggest you painstakingly go through the past three months of all your accounts. List all the regular debits/payments. The main objective here is to get an idea of how much is really leaving your account every month and becoming conscious of what those items are.

Chances are you'll find items in the same category that you're doubling up on. For example, I was given a free Apple Music subscription for 18 months last time I upgraded my phone (thanks Telstra!). However, we were already paying for Spotify, which offers a very similar service. The same goes for Foxtel, Stan, Netflix, Apple TV and Disney+! What other apps are you paying for that you don't use?

## Start a side-hustle

You've got 24 hours a day. Time to turn off the Kardashians and hustle like a momager! Do some freelance writing, drive for Uber, be a maths tutor or an online dating consultant (they exist!) — there are millions of ideas here. Get off the couch and use the time you've been given. Any extra cash can go straight to paying off your debt.

## Lose the gym membership

This is one of the biggest but most underutilised expenses in my clients' budgets. There are cheaper ways to exercise. The ocean is my gym but if that's not your vibe, go for a run, use the gym at the park or Google outdoor or home gym exercise ideas. For some people the gym is non-negotiable, which is cool. But if you choose to spend money in one particular area, make sure you seriously value it. Ramit Sethi, who's a true genius when it comes to personal money coaching, advocates saving mercilessly on the items that don't mean anything to you, so you can then spend wildly on the one or two that do. If the gym is your solace and safe place for staying fit, then go for it! Just make sure it's intentional and you review it every now and then.

## Utilise the sharing economy

Airbnb your home, even if you're renting. If you have a spare room or two, make the most of it. Do this permanently, or at least whenever you go on holidays, even if it's just a long weekend visiting family. You have to be a bit organised but it's all worth it. We've done this with our place a few times. One year it funded almost an entire three-week trip to the US!

Share your car. There are a bunch of great sharing sites like Uber Carshare (previously Car Next Door) that are super easy to use and a great way to earn some extra coin from your gas guzzler. Better still, sell your car and use Go Get or another sharing service. I have a few clients who use this and absolutely rave about it.

If you haven't written out all your expenses, scan the QR code on page 48 and we'll send you our template. It will prompt all of this and be the starting point for your spending plan, coming up soon.

## Move back home

Your parents will kill me, but I have definitely seen many people create this win to avoid rising rents and allow for enough surplus either to significantly reduce debt or to build up a savings buffer. Just make sure it's a temporary move. I didn't write this book for 45-year-olds who enjoy sitting on their arses. Your independence matters more in the long run, but paying off debt is a short-term issue so deal with it first. Plus, who doesn't love Mum's lasagne!

## Negotiate a remote/virtual work arrangement and drop the commute

At Sufficient Funds we run what Matt Mullenweg of Wordpress fame would call a distributed business. We're not strictly 'remote', as this would imply we have a head office with staff working remotely from HQ. These days I have no interest in having a shiny office in the big smoke. Our team of awesome humans all work from home, some globally, and we freakin' love it. We're now conducting 100 per cent of our meetings via video. This allows us to work with driven young peeps all over Australia, and they don't need to leave their homes!

It also means we can live wherever we want to and still be doing the work we love, simultaneously showing our kids how others live, letting them learn from these new ways, and giving them an insight into the amazing diversity on this planet.

Businesses globally were forced by the pandemic into being open to this concept. You get more done in less time, save on travel costs and create more flexibility around important family tasks like childcare. What's more, you're allowed to open the windows without being concerned about someone else's climate-controlled nightmare, and PJs (even pants off Fridays!) are fully permitted.

Money nerd talking: you might also get to claim some of your rent or mortgage as tax deductible, but get appropriate tax advice from a good accountant.

We live in a global society. Just as many others have done before you, embrace it and see where it takes you.

## Live somewhere cheaper

City living is ridiculously expensive in comparison to regional areas. Either commute further (and spend the travel time on your side-hustle or listening to podcasts!), work remotely or set up a virtual business like ours, so you can be location independent and remove the impulse spending distractions that are so prevalent in big cities.

## Don't cut the holiday—turn it into a savings opportunity

Everyone needs regular breaks to relax, dream bigger and reset. In line with your definition of Sufficient, think about what you need for a holiday to be enjoyable and tick your true value boxes. This might involve finding cheaper places to travel, getting away from the five-star resorts that may have got you into this mess in the first place. Staying in hostels can be a great way to meet people and see the world.

Planning ahead and booking your holidays 12 to 18 months in advance can score you some serious deals, leaving more money in your pocket to spend on experiences and creating memories that last a lifetime. Time to lock in that Icelandic adventure. Thank me later!

## ACTIVITY
## Disrupt your debts

Take one hour to act on the practical tips above. Grab your laptop and review all of your transactional bank account statements, focusing on 'foiling fraudsters' and 'finding double-ups'. This will give further insight into any other expenses you could be removing from your life.

I've given you a few other ideas to help you get creative around this. Spend some time thinking about how all of these or other ideas specific to your life could work to disrupt your debt and bring you back onto the path to Sufficient Funds.

**Note:** If you're in a serious mess financially and you've tried all of the above, then it's time to speak to a financial counsellor. There are some free options out there that do amazing work and can definitely point you in the right direction. In Australia, start with the Commonwealth Government's Moneysmart site or the National Debt Helpline. You can also try local councils in metro areas or many charities who are set up to assist, such as the Salvation Army or the Smith Family.

# Cruise Control: Your Spending Plan

Your spending plan is hands down the most crucial part to get right. An effective spending plan has two key elements: the right behaviour and the right system. In *Atomic Habits*, author James Clear notes, 'You do not rise to the level of your goals, you fall to the level of your systems.'

When striving for flow we need as little friction as possible. This means building systems for money decisions and maintaining pure clarity on how those decisions link to your best life. It also means you don't second guess a thing. You need the tools to make quick, confident, intentional decisions, and move on.

There's no room here for dwelling on the past and getting stuck on the negatives. Your success is predicated on your ability to progress.

I'm going to show you a structure and foolproof system that works for all the awesome clients we get to work with every day, and why it is the basis of all successful financial plans.

The four key components to 'Cruise Control: Your Spending Plan' are:

- Budget

- Categorise

- Accounts

- Automate.

## Budget

It starts with that dirty B word. There's no doubt this is the reason so many people fail at the first hurdle of sorting their money out. Don't sweat, I'm on your page with this! I've already made my disdain for extreme frugality very clear and I promise I'm here to make this palatable for you. So stay with me, because this is the next crucial step to achieving Sufficient Funds.

A budget allows you to understand your 'cost of living'. To be financially successful, and to fast-track your journey to Sufficient, you need to know what it costs to be you. One thing's for sure: when I keep a budget I have more money, even though I'm not earning any more.

I'll never tell you what to spend your money on; however, it's about being conscious of what's coming and going, and more than anything it's about aligning your spending with your values.

One benefit of spending the time upfront defining Sufficient and encouraging you to think bigger is that motivation and clarity make the whole idea of budgeting so much easier to stomach. Once you nail this part you'll see how to build the plan that brings it all together!

## ACTIVITY
## Complete your budget template

Scan the QR code to download the budget template. This will prompt everything for you. Spend 20 to 30 minutes completing this. Most of it will be fixed costs that you will already know or can easily find in your statements; the rest you'll need to give some thought to.

*Bonus tip:* Here's exactly what we tell clients when they complete this with us: fill this with everything you think you're spending at the moment, plus anything you wish you could be spending money on! If there's anything missing in your life that you want more of, add it into the budget and let's work together to make it happen! We can always reduce it later if needed.

# ACTIVITY
# Get comfortable talking about spending money...like, today!

If you're a couple and have shared income, bank accounts, expenditure, make sure you have made the time and effort to get on the same page about money.

Ideally this came up naturally when you defined Sufficient, but if you're just now starting to get on the same page with your budget, you're going to want to start with aligning your spending philosophies. I have seen people avoid completing their budget, revisiting their budget or even looking at their bank accounts as they don't want to either start arguments or divulge spending they think their partner might not be on board with. We're all human and we all have different wants and needs. Talk it out and don't let this be the thing that sets you back.

If all else fails, agree to disagree on selected budget items, but know what that means for your financial position and your ongoing comfort level. As Jim Carrey said, 'Behind every great man is a woman rolling her eyes.'

## Categorise

I'm not a fan of over-engineering things. You're here to declutter and you don't need 1000 bank accounts.

At the same time, though, the super-simple, one account for all income, expenses and savings is just as bad in my opinion. One account and one credit card generally isn't enough. You want clarity over your costs and an easy way to see how you're progressing between pays without tracking every cent you spend.

We follow a very simple split of categories. Either it's fun or it's boring. You have living costs (boring) and lifestyle costs (fun). Another way to think about this is that living costs are not really discretionary; that is, you can't really live without them, or at least you've made the decision that they're essential in your life. Lifestyle costs are based on discretionary choices made based on what makes you happy, but in an emergency you could drop or cut back on most of these if needed.

Here are a few common examples:

- Living (boring):
  - Groceries and takeaway (we view takeaway as a necessity [boring] as opposed to eating out [fun])
  - education/childcare
  - insurance
  - transport
  - loan repayments
  - pet expenses (our clients and team take pet ownership as seriously as children, so for most these are not just lifestyle decisions)
  - donations
- Lifestyle (fun):
  - entertainment — movies, concerts, zoo tickets

- eating out

- looking good — clothes, beautician, hairdresser, Botox

- subscriptions

- travel

- gifts

- personal spending — handbags, golf clubs, surfboards

---

**A note on subscriptions:** We used to call this a living cost but this has become a watch-out for a lot of people. It's easy to fall into the trap of collecting these ever-multiplying services (for example Binge, Kayo, Netflix, Disney+, Stan, Apple TV). I've seen clients spending over $250 per month on these, where they thought it was only $50. Again, I'm not here to tell you what to spend on, but check yourself if it's getting a little wild, and drop the ones you're not using right now. You can pick them up later if needed; that's the beauty of 'no contracts'!

---

## Accounts

The account structure aligns with the categories above, with a few extra splits for specific and common goals.

I meet people all the time who tell me one of many versions of this: 'James, I feel like I earn way too much to have this little.' Figure 2.2 (overleaf) introduces a couple of case studies (names removed to protect the innocent!).

| Client 1 | | Client 2 |
|---|---|---|
| Single, 39 years old | | Couple, mid to late forties |
| No dependents | | Two kids finished private school |
| Renting | | Paying the minimum repayment on a highly manageable $700k mortgage |
| Earning $240k p.a. income, earning similar money for at least the past five years. | | $485k p.a. combined income, not contributing any additional funds to super or investments |
| $40 000 savings built up over five years, $150 000 super balance (average for this age and income) | | Living mainly off a credit card, paying it off annually when a bonus comes in |

**Figure 2.2: Client case studies—'earning too much to have so little'**

These are two very different examples. We can help some of our clients towards huge wins very quickly but most, who are neither extreme spenders nor excessively frugal, fall somewhere in the middle, and I'm guessing you're among them. What you need is a simple set of accounts (see figures 2.3 and 2.4) that align with your ideal life so you can go and live it!

## Your account types

| DAY-TO-DAY ACCOUNTS | UPCOMING ACCOUNTS | SQUIRREL ACCOUNTS |
|---|---|---|
| **Everyday spending**<br>• Bills and expenses<br>• Personal spending<br>• Regular lifestyle spending | **Future spending <12 mths**<br>• Holidays/travel account<br>• Irregular entertainment<br>• Presents/gifts | **Savings and paying off loans**<br>• Home deposit/ renovation account<br>• Home loans<br>• Investment accounts<br>• Maxed credit cards<br>• Emergency fund<br>• Parental/baby fund |

**Figure 2.3: Your account types**

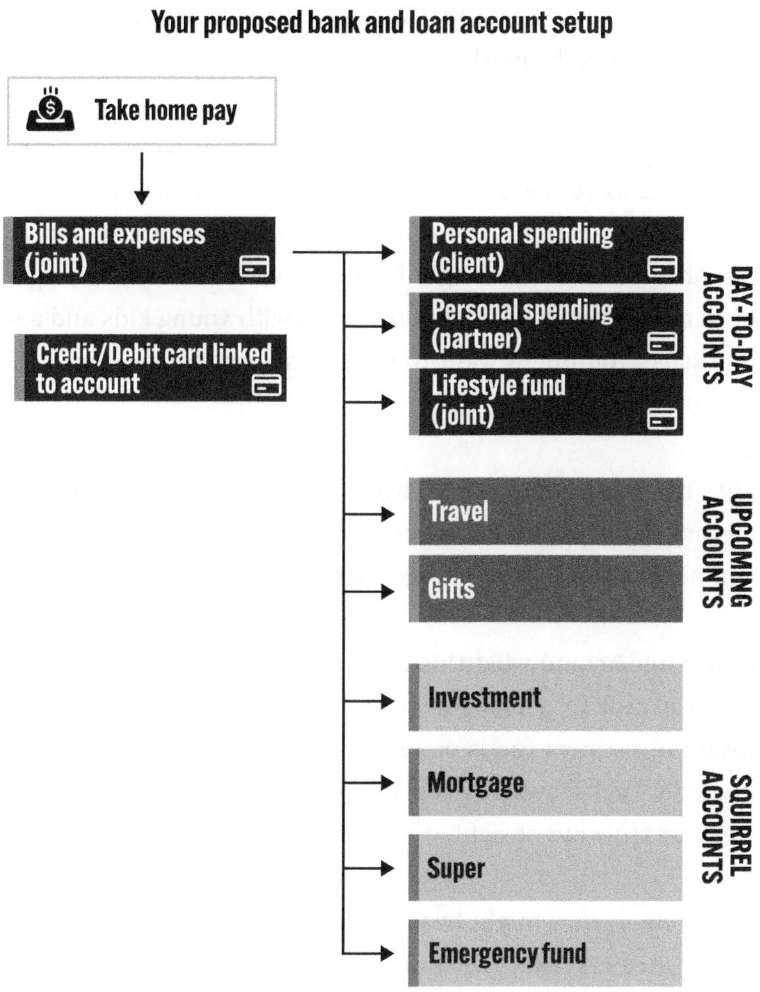

## Your proposed bank and loan account setup

Figure 2.4: Your flow of funds

## 1. EMERGENCY FUND

You've likely heard about this before. Scott Pape, the 'Barefoot Investor', recommends three months of living expenses, which is perhaps a good starting point, but the difficulty with giving very specific advice like this to a very diverse readership is that it will inevitably miss the mark with most.

A Sufficient emergency fund has just enough. Too little is risky, too much means you're missing opportunities to invest or enjoy more of your hard-earned. If you're single with a secure income, two months of living costs might be fine. If you're newly self-employed or in a highly volatile contractual role, with young kids and a solid mortgage, you might want to up it to six months or even a whole year of expenses.

I like nice round numbers, so whether it's $5000 or $100 000 make it an easy number and don't overthink. Crucially, I want you to adapt a mindset around your emergency fund that it's not your money!

Please understand what this fund represents: it's money you never touch except in a real financial emergency. Don't think of it as future investment funds or some extra dosh for the next furniture upgrade. Tuck it away, even at a separate bank if you need to, so it's well and truly out of sight, out of mind.

A real emergency might be that you lose your job, you face big and urgent medical costs, the family business slows right down, you find yourself between contracts for much longer than expected, or your parents or kids find themselves stuck overseas.

For us, our son Eden spent his first three months in and out of hospital. He was born only 11 days after our SF business was launched. Tash had deferred her employer's parental leave (for tax purposes, of course) and we had to park everything, lay low and spend another three months picking up the pieces before it all started to flow again.

Chapter 4 dives into events like this, but for now, completing this step sets you up to return to the good times much faster.

I've spoken about the importance of mindset. Setting up an emergency fund is one key way to gain peace of mind. It gives you comfort and clarity around your buffer, so you can progress more confidently and swiftly towards Sufficient Funds.

Here's a super-common new client conversation.

> *Me:* So tell me about what you're dealing with at the moment. Do you have debts, savings? What does this all look like for you?
>
> *You:* I'm debt free now apart from HECS, so I'm building my emergency fund and saving for my next holiday. I invest $200 a month in ETFs (more on these in chapter 3), oh and I have about $10 000 in a separate account for other savings.
>
> *Me:* Okay, so what's your 'other savings' for specifically?
>
> *You:* Nothing really, it's just there in case I need it.
>
> *Me:* So where is your emergency fund up to now?
>
> *You:* I have $3200 right now, and I want to get it to $10 000.

It's very common for new clients to tell us they're squirrelling funds away for a higher purpose before they have built a full emergency fund. If you don't have any personal debt (such as Buy Now Pay Later (BNPL), credit card or unsecured personal loans), but your emergency fund is not yet at a level you're comfortable with, my general rule is you should not focus on anything but filling this up!

# Day-to-day accounts

Let's break down all the accounts you're going to need day-to-day.

## 2. BILLS AND EXPENSES

This is the new engine room for your finances! Ideally, whether you're single, a couple or have a massive family, keep one account for bills. Everyone should have debit card access. Label your cards and remember which is which for tapping your phone, as you'll also have one or two more cards for the fun stuff.

All income goes in here (your salary and any dividends or rental income). All living expenses go through here. If you have a credit card, pay it off, ideally in full, from this account each pay. Tap, EFT or BPAY all living expense bills from this account.

Working on combining finances for the first time? This is a great place to start as you'll find a lot of these are joint costs. If you're not ready to have both incomes coming into the same joint account and want to keep things 'even', try agreeing on a fixed amount each pay that is transferred into this one for all joint costs. Don't force it. If you're not both ready to do this, it's not urgent. You'll know when the time is right.

**Card access required:** YES
**Starting balance before pay lands:** One month's 'living' costs (from Tab 2 in the budget template, not lifestyle).

## 3. LIFESTYLE

All lifestyle costs, as previously categorised. No bills.

**Card access required:** YES
**For couples/families:** JOINT
**Starting balance before pay lands:** $0

## 4. PERSONAL SPENDING (FUN)

Skip this one if you're single or in a relationship and comfortable having everything joint. This is about decluttering! Don't confuse yourself with extra accounts if you don't need them.

Having said that, however, a lot of couples we work with choose to have a separate 'fun' or 'personal spending' account each. This allows complete guilt-free spending at a pre-agreed level. It also means you can sneak in presents for each other without it being too obvious!

If you're at the pub together or out for a nice romantic dinner, you're spending from the joint lifestyle fund above. Heels on and running solo with the ladies? Use this one.

I've seen anything from $50 to $1000 a week go into this account. It will come down to your income level and how expensive your definition of fun is. Again, if it's affordable, and everything else is flowing in the right direction, then I won't judge you here. Just remember to align it with your values.

**Card access required:** YES
**Starting balance before pay lands:** $0

# *Upcoming accounts*

## 5. TRAVEL

Our favourite pot of gold! Maybe you have a massive European or US trip coming up, or perhaps you're more of a homebody targeting the occasional weekend away. Whatever this is for you, I suggest you keep it separate and when you transfer in here, it is 'assumed spent'. Gone. This allows for 100 per cent guilt-free travel! Don't mess with this, as for most of the legends we work with, this is highly valued, away-from-work, get-creative, reset, realign, relax time … you get it!

Separating out this money forces you to align your behaviour with your goal. When you're living day-to-day and have had a few extra splurges, you've been a bit loose with your spending and your day-to-day accounts are approaching \$0, or you need to pull money from your 'Niseko powder' or 'Barossa with the girls' stash, you're definitely going to think twice about blowing those extra funds. This is why we 'Define' first. Ensure your goals are motivating enough to keep your money plan on track!

**Card access required:** NO. (I repeat, NO!) There is no way you want to be able to access this stash on a whim without taking a good, hard look at yourself.
**Starting balance before pay lands:** \$0 if not travelling for 12 months.

Here's the real trick if you're up for it. You've heard people talk about booking a holiday from a holiday? Well, here's how. Loosely calculate your next 18 to 24 months of travel plans and begin with however much you need for the current year's spend. That way you're now saving for next year's holidays and really getting ahead!

Coming out of COVID-related lockdowns with a fully stacked travel fund felt pretty good. One of the benefits of a less adventurous two years.

## 6. GIFTS

This is without a doubt the most commonly underestimated item in our clients' budgets, and it was a surprise for us personally until we stopped and made our own list. Tash and I tend to be fairly generous when it comes to buying presents. I think this is fine, but it adds up quickly, especially if you have a big family, a bunch of nieces and nephews, or if you're in the 25- to 35-year-old 'wedding zone'. Typically I suggest you list everyone you'd like to be buying for, break it down by birthdays and holidays, then add the other likely ad hoc items like engagements, weddings and other specific cultural celebrations.

If you think you spend only $1000 a year on gifts, my guess is you may need to more than double that. When we first did this, our list quickly added up to more than $5000 p.a. Totally fine if you can afford it, and it's something you value, but worth a squiz just in case.

**Card access required:** NO
**Starting balance before pay lands:** $0 (or 50 per cent of your annual spend if it's past June and the holiday season is approaching)

It may help to have other 'Upcoming' or 'Squirrel' accounts (we've seen it all, and some of these may be very relevant to you!):

- **Baby.** Saving to start a family — more on this in chapter 4.

- **Family support.** Helping parents or other family members financially.

- **Car.** Paying the balloon/residual value on a car loan and keeping the car.

- **Home renovations.** For minor upgrades, not major renos where you're generally extending the home loan.

- **Shooting-through fund.** Sadly this will be a reality for many, including those suffering financial or domestic abuse. Having a back-up account in your own name outside of the emergency fund could be critical.

- **Financial freedom fund.** Helping you leverage your time to spend it aligned to your definition of Sufficient — more on this in chapter 3.

For some people, keeping separate accounts for each of these extras works best. Others are comfortable storing at least some of the different squirrel funds in one account. This is quite common if you're using an offset account with your home loan and are trying to achieve a higher interest saving. Again, though, if combining funds becomes confusing and more time-consuming, you'll be more likely to overspend, so don't get stuck chasing the interest saving when structure, which drives behaviour, beats interest saving every day of the week. When in doubt, silo your money, name accounts accordingly and keep it flowing!

# Automate

Got the accounts sorted? Time to make it FLOW! You are human, don't let this fact ruin your big plans. The point of automating is to remove you from the system by following these steps in order:

## 1. STARTING BALANCE TO BILLS ACCOUNT

Wait until you're about to get paid and add your starting balance to the Bills account. This starting balance gives you a full month's buffer.

## 2. DIRECT DEBITS FOR EVERYTHING WHERE POSSIBLE

Use your budget to question every single expense: can this be automated? This includes the obvious ones like rent, mortgage and utilities, but also those sneaky quarterly bills like council and water rates. Complete a direct debit application on the provider's site (for some regional councils you'll need to call or email). If you find it easier to manage shorter billing cycles, split these up into monthly payments.

You'll find almost all of your direct debits come from your Bills account, which is why you have a month's buffer here and it receives all of your income.

## 3. AUTOMATIC TRANSFERS TO EACH OF YOUR OTHER ACCOUNTS

From your Bills account, you now need to set up automatic transfers to each of your other accounts according to your budget and goals. Line up the frequency of transfers with your pay cycle and set up the auto-transfer to leave Bills the day after your pay lands just to be sure.

If you've downloaded our budget template, this is easy. Tab 2 gives you all of the numbers required here for weekly, fortnightly or monthly cycles. Otherwise, simply take your total annual spend and divide by 52 (weekly), 26 (fortnightly) or 12 (monthly).

## 4. AUTOMATE YOUR INVESTMENTS

Hopefully you're now starting to see the cascading effect of this process — making your money truly flow. From here you can start to make direct automated payments into your chosen investments, so not only are all your spending bases covered, but you are intentionally making your money work for you in a hands-free way.

We'll talk about investing in chapter 3.

You're killing it! Everything is now automated and you're creating some incredible habits that will set you up for financial success.

Before you move on ... CELEBRATE! It's time to celebrate your wins. It can be hard work to get in the mental zone to sort your money out. Be super proud of what you've achieved and acknowledge it with high fives, tequila shots or whatever works for you!

# FAQs

*But I use my credit card for everything!*
I'm not against credit cards, but they're not for everyone and I've seen them ruin some of the best-laid plans. If you're just getting started with your spending plan and are not yet in full 'cruise control', I'd be leaving the credit card right out of the equation. Put yourself on L-plates for now, and gain full confidence over using *your* money in your day-to-day accounts. The learned behaviour and habits you develop from this are crucial to achieving Sufficient Funds.

Be very careful with the 'spending for points' argument too. Rewards points are not worth what they used to be, and even the slightest amount of overspending chasing status or points bonuses very rarely translates into a smart financial decision and will undo some of the other great work you're now doing.

When might a credit card for rewards points actually be helpful? Usually when it's already part of a mortgage package where the fee you're paying is outweighed by the benefit of at least one offset account. It may also be useful when you spend on it for large items you've already saved for, such as international travel, and you immediately transfer from your travel account (or other relevant account) to pay off the purchase, without paying interest. This can work as long as you're in cruise control with the rest of the above. If in doubt, leave it out.

*Can't I just invest already?*
Not everyone we start working with is super engaged with their money, and that's totally normal. However, lots of our SF clients are. What can result from this is a burning desire to do everything at once. Everyone wants the spicy, exciting part, but TBH you need to hit your emergency fund target first and lock it away in a separate cash account removed from your day-to-day accounts. Get this done before you start dripping your surplus into investments or saving for your property deposit.

*What if I start with cruise control and leave the debt for now?*
Please don't. You'll feel a much greater sense of achievement if you tick off this all-important, and annoying AF pain in your life.

This is your chance to change the course of your life forever, and putting in the hard yards now will make all the difference. Also, investing without an emergency fund means if an emergency does occur in your life, you're then at the mercy of having your cash in a higher-risk environment and of it not being there the day you desperately need it.

*Can I start with zero dollars?*
Starting with $0 is perfect. You're not alone. It's the structure that's so crucial here, not the amounts in it. If close to $0 is your current reality, this new system for your money will help ensure you're giving yourself every chance of future financial success, even if you're not feeling it right now.

## ACTIVITY
## Get off the couch and get money fit by doing one or two of these each week:

- Automate your bills, including quarterly and annual bills.

- Make sure bills are emailed not posted.

- Turf all the paper, scanning the important things using Evernote.

- Close unnecessary bank accounts.

- Consolidate debts.

- Consolidate super, but don't do this without being certain you don't need the insurance inside your super funds. If in doubt, seek financial advice here before acting. This is a common error we see, and generally not one that can be undone.

- Automate your savings.

- Review insurance policies.

- Review bank statements for unnecessary memberships or subscriptions you no longer use.

## Sufficiently Decluttered

By the end of this chapter:

- As in every other area of life that matters, you understand the importance of clarity and focus when dealing with your finances.

- You have a list of all your debts and have begun to snowball or avalanche these the hell out of your life forever!

- You've completed your budget with your net income and every possible weekly, monthly and annual expense, as well as any additional spending in line with your new list of goals from chapter 1.

- You've set up an emergency fund and have a good grasp of exactly how much money you need in this account.

- You've categorised all spending using your budget template, set up your account structure and renamed your accounts online.

- You've set up automation on your accounts so your money flows exactly as intended, without getting in your own way and messing it up.

Hell yeah! You did it! Extra congrats if this is totally not your everyday jam. We see all types in the clients we work with and I know you're either loving this or somehow forcing yourself through it anyway. Either way you're not alone and I'm bloody proud of the fact that you're now taking charge and controlling your future.

Don't forget the final step of celebrating your new decluttered money status ... you've earned it!

You're clear and focused and fully understand your cash in and cash out. This lines you up perfectly for developing your growth strategy!

Now it's time to answer the question that will help you dial this up big time: *Where does what you have left over go?*

# CHAPTER THREE

# Develop—big plans, growth and mad momentum

Congratulations! Now you've cleared the decks by decluttering your finances, it's time to step it up. You're on cruise control with your spending plan and have a clear idea of how much should be left over. It's time to develop your growth strategy!

I touched on this earlier, the concept that true happiness comes from progress and growth. It's a part of our biology that's hard to deny. While it is valuable to pause and reflect, we're at our best when we're not standing still for too long.

When Tash and I sorted our spending, decluttered our finances and turned our efforts towards growth, we knew we needed a solid plan. We wanted to develop and improve ourselves as fast as possible, understanding that this was the key to earning more and building the life we wanted. But we also needed to be super strategic as the financial elements started to come together. We needed to understand our own appetite for risk, both as individuals and as a couple, and we needed to have enough financial literacy to make sure we were channelling funds into smart investments.

In chapter 3, I'll cover a bunch of areas you will need to be on top of in order to build your money life in a way that puts you on the fast track to Sufficient Funds. We're accelerating from bank accounts to investment options; I'll debunk a major tax myth that has so many treading water; and I'll introduce a new way of thinking about your super fund.

Before we get stuck into investment options, it's time to blow the lid off one of the core elements of our work with clients at Sufficient Funds and explain the concept of the four stacks of Sufficient Funds.

---

**Note:** I've aimed to break down most of the technical stuff in this book. You will already know that the financial industry is like any other, wittingly or unwittingly confusing everyone through the massive overuse of acronyms, abbreviations and other jargon. One thing we avoid at all costs in our business is using these bewildering terms with our clients. We get it. It's hard enough to build up the courage to approach a financial planner and open up to the opportunity ahead of you without the fear of being 'talked at' about your own damn money and left more confused than when you started.

---

# The 'mad stacks' strategy: introducing the four stacks of Sufficient Funds

Now you've decluttered your finances, you should be very familiar with what's coming in and what's going out. If you have a decent chunk of money left over after each pay, congratulations! You probably look financially similar to most of our clients when they first engage with us. You're also likely to face the issue of knowing what to do with the extra funds.

Of course, having options is a great challenge to have; in fact, it's one we all strive for, but it is still a challenge, and one that should not be taken lightly. One wrong step could cost you tens of thousands of dollars, more years of work or, worse, the inability to achieve Sufficient Funds and the goals and dreams you set out in chapter 1.

Even if you do all the research and spend the time to understand the technical aspects of the financial choices available to you, there's still the matter of getting out of your own way and making the right decision — or rather, all the right decisions. And you need to get the sequence of these decisions right too.

Fortunately, there's an easy way to think about this, and it involves the idea of *four stacks*.

This is where the rubber really hits the road for our clients, and where we add massive value to their lives. I'm going to lay it all out for you right here.

The four stacks are very simple. They are:

1. Debts

2. Savings

3. Investment

4. Super.

At any point in time you would rarely be targeting only one stack. In fact, I would argue that unless you're swimming in the types of debts we discussed in chapter 2 (credit cards, personal loans or BNPL), you're likely to need at least two or three of the stacks at all times. Think of this as literal stacks of cash on the table in front of you, but with very specific rules and purposes for each.

Those on a decent income with HECS/HELP or a mortgage, a chunk of spare cash and 20 to 30 years before retirement will probably want to make use of all four stacks of Sufficient Funds, just like Nicola.

## A client example

Nicola is single, 32 years old, a medical doctor on an income of $220000 with $150000 in savings.

- **Stack 1 (Debt):** She made a large payment to her significant HELP debt last year, saving a one-off indexation of 7.2 per cent. She also extinguished some annoying Afterpay debt that she didn't realise was costing her a heap, even on a low balance of approximately $2000.

- **Stack 2 (Savings):** Nicola is funnelling $1500 per month into her travel fund. Her number one ongoing priority is what she calls 'adventure', and she is actively spending this in one to two epic trips per year. She also just finished saving $8000 to fund freezing her eggs (more on this in the next chapter), as well as funding some of her future home deposit with savings in the bank.

- **Stack 3 (Investment):** With her work, Nicola has the ongoing need to be flexible around which city or state she lives in. She wants to stay open to all opportunities, but renting and being debt free are key flexibility factors. She is saving approximately $5000 a month, and to help fund her house deposit she is now investing 50 per cent of this in a parcel of managed funds (read more about different ways to invest in the share market later in this section). The idea here is she is spreading her surplus cash between share investment (a growth asset with more risk, but likely more return over five to seven years or more) and bank savings (cash is a defensive asset, with little or no risk but a likely lower return).

- **Stack 4 (Super):** The final portion of her cash is now being utilised in the First Home Super Saver Scheme (FHSS). As a first home buyer, she is able to contribute $50000 under the FHSS, at a maximum of $15000 per annum. She is going to make concessional (pre-tax) contributions to super of $15000 for the next three financial years, and one final contribution of $5000. She is doing this as soon as possible, rather than spreading it over five or more years, because the deemed rate of return inside super under the FHSS is higher than the savings rate paid by banks and therefore a more attractive yet still very safe option for her.

# A note on super contributions

**There are two ways to contribute to super:** concessionally or non-concessionally, each with its own limits and tax treatment.

*Concessional contributions* are pre-tax. These include both personal contributions you make before tax and Superannuation Guarantee Contributions (SGC—the ones the government makes your employer do, is 11.5 per cent of your income as of July 2024, before rising to 12 per cent from July 2025).

To make a pre-tax contribution you can either instruct your employer to start a 'salary sacrifice' to super for you, which will come out of each pay before tax is taken out, or you can do this manually by using the BPAY details provided by your super fund. If you make a manual contribution to super, you will need to complete an ATO form called a notice of intent, which is lodged with your super fund to ensure you get the tax benefit. Concessional contributions are taxed at a lower rate inside super (15 per cent, or 30 per cent for income earned over $250 000) than most people's marginal tax rate and currently have a limit of $30 000 per annum including SGC.

*Non-concessional contributions* are made after tax, meaning you have already paid tax on it before you choose to add it to super. There is no tax on this money when it lands in super. The current limit to these contributions is $110 000 per annum. If you have a larger amount to contribute you can send a whole three years' worth, or up to $333 000, using what is known as the 'bring-forward rule'. This strategy is more common with those closer to retirement or for younger peeps after the sale of a significant asset like a business or property and less pressure on the other three stacks (usually own home, debt-free, cash-sufficient and investments solid).

As soon as Nicola has maxed out her $50000 contributed towards the FHSS she plans to continue contributing at a lower rate to max out her concessional (pre-tax) contributions cap. At that point her debt stack will become the mortgage, and super will be utilised solely for a long-term, tax-free retirement income. More on super, and why it should matter a lot to you right now, soon.

You may have picked up on the fact that Nicola is currently putting more into super than her annual concessional contributions cap allows. At the time of writing the cap is $30000 and her employer pays her Super Guarantee Contributions of $24420 simply because she earns $220000 and this is currently legislated at 11.5 per cent. So when she adds $15000 of her own contribution to this she is blowing the annual cap out of the water by $9420. The good news is that she is able to benefit from the 'carry-forward' contribution rules. As she doesn't yet have $500000 in super, and her income increased significantly recently, she has a lot more room to move with her previous year's caps, which she can now utilise to top up her super fund for the FHSS and still benefit from the tax deductions available as a result. WINNING!

Remember, you don't need to extinguish all debts before you start investing!

Bad debt should absolutely be zeroed before tackling anything other than creating a small emergency fund. Other debts, however — in particular any educational loans such as HECS/HELP, your mortgage and any investment loans — and the decision to pay these down faster than the contracted minimum repayments, should become part of your greater strategy and one of your options in terms of where you direct surplus funds each pay cycle. Just because you have a mortgage doesn't mean you shouldn't be investing or potentially contributing to super.

Of course, the specifics of how this applies to you, compared with the next individual, couple or family, will vary dramatically based on your goals, your target timeframes for these and the flexibility of these if something goes wrong.

One way to think about it is as 'return on investment', or ROI as we money nerds know it. Your ROI is most easily thought of as a percentage. If I invest $100 today, and it's worth $107 in 12 months' time, I've made an ROI of 7 per cent for the year it's been invested.

When it comes to adding cash to your debt stack, I want you to think about your ROI as how much you will save, and for the other three (savings, investment, super) as how much you will make. You can then use the resulting percentage as a way of comparing the benefit. Let's go a bit deeper. Your ROI for directing your spare cash to debt is equal to the interest rate on the debt you are paying off; for example, if you have a home loan with a rate of 6 per cent, then adding cash to this (paying it down) saves you 6 per cent. With investments your ROI is either the income or the growth (increase in value over time), or both. For example, the ROI of cash in the bank is equal to the interest rate received; however, the ROI for an investment in shares is equal to the growth in value plus the income received (more on income from shares, or dividends, coming up).

If it's HELP/HECS debt, then the ROI is a little more unpredictable. In Australia this debt is indexed each year at the start of June for all debt that has been outstanding for more than 11 months. Indexation means the government applies a percentage increase to the debt, just as a bank applies interest to a loan. Therefore, when thinking about paying off HELP/HECS your ROI is equal to the indexation percentage, announced each year around April or May.

Note that tax implications also need to be taken into account when calculating ROI. I cover tax in more detail later in the chapter, but for now, just know that the interest on a debt used to purchase an asset that generates investment income, for example an investment property loan, may be tax deductible to you. So your ROI of paying off an investment debt vs an owner-occupied home loan with no tax benefits is going to be different. Your ROI for paying off the investment debt will be reduced by the amount of tax benefit you miss out on, where for the owner-occupied loan your ROI remains at the interest rate of the loan itself.

Investment returns are also taxable. Income is generally taxed in your annual tax return, where tax on growth is paid in the year that you sell an asset and realise a 'capital gain' — hence the term capital gains tax (CGT).

It would be nice if all you had to think about when it comes to building your stacks is the ROI. There's a bit more to it, though!

Another important factor in deciding which stack to target, especially for the savings, investment or super stacks, is the timeframe you have until you need the cash. If your goal is to retire with stacks of tax-free income available to you, and there are no other major goals standing in your way, then you'll be okay to pump your super fund as hard as possible, ensuring you do this in a tax-effective way.

For our clients, most of whom are between 25 and 45 years old, major goals are a fact of life! They commonly include more pets, starting a family, multiple and significant adventures, buying their first home, supporting kids with big purchases and education, flexible work, starting a business, home upgrade and early retirement.

Finally, your need for cash will depend on the flexibility of the goal itself. If your goal is to upgrade your home to a nicer suburb closer to the beach, you might say that ideally this goal will happen in the next three years, but if it was to happen in year four or five, that would also be okay. However, the goal of putting your child through private schooling for high school does not have a flexible timeline. You can't delay when the beginning of year seven comes flying around!

# The right amount in each stack!

I've already covered this in theory, but here's the detail. Your key to achieving Sufficient Funds is having your money decisions fully aligned to the life you want to live and to be confidently on track for all of it!

Take our client Nicola. In six years, with a new home and a mortgage, and likely a long-term partner in her life, here's how this could play out:

- *Debt*: She will extinguish her new home loan within 15 years. A simple online mortgage calculator allowed her to set the goal of paying it off during this time, allowing a buffer for higher interest rates, and she has automated the additional repayments.

- *Savings*: With the help of our mortgage broking team, she found a loan structure that allows multiple offset accounts, which means she can save cash according to Cruise Control: Your Spending Plan, and have every cent she accumulates offsetting interest on her mortgage. This is one way to make your money really work for you.

- Her emergency fund is full. Her adventure fund is also full. In fact, not only has she prepaid her upcoming month in Argentina, but she's a year ahead with this. This allows her to book her next adventure from the last one so she always has something to look forward to.

- She and her partner Jake are actively planning to start a family. They're jointly saving to their baby fund, allowing them enough to get through the income fluctuations of having two children and each of them going back to working four days a week (see chapter 4 for how you can do this).

- *Investment*: As soon as she had enough money in her house deposit fund, she shifted her thinking around her investment portfolio to the longer term. This has become her future financial freedom fund, allowing flexibility around how much she works from age 50 or 55 onwards. This stack will reach sufficient height when it can generate an annual $500 000 of additional income, so she's investing enough to get this to $1 million. This allows her to significantly reduce her work hours, or even stop work if she wants to, once the mortgage has been paid off, and it gets her safely to her preservation age (In short, when she can access super, discussed later in this chapter).

> **Note:** For calculating passive income (in this case, income derived from investments that you don't have to work for, or even better, that allow you to stop working!), use a 5 per cent return and, if invested well, you shouldn't need to eat into your capital (your investment balance remains intact): $1 000 000 generates $50 000 p.a. income forever. In your head, simply remove a zero and divide by 2:
>
> $1 000 000 → (remove zero) → $100 000 → (divide x 2) → $50 000

- *Super*: After successfully utilising the FHSS for part of her home deposit, being on track to pay out the mortgage and be financially flexible in her early 50s, she now has a clear runway to starting to really pump her super fund.

To summarise the four stacks of Sufficient Funds philosophy: you will generally have a few stacks that you're piling into simultaneously, all driven by their ROI, your main goals and their desired timeframes.

From the top, once Debt is taken care of (that is, you have no bad debt, and remaining debt, such as mortgage, investment, education and car loan, is on track for the desired timeframe), focus on Savings. Once your cash needs are on track to be sufficiently stacked, then you can think about pumping Investment. Investment and Super can be pumped simultaneously. If your investment stacks are on track to handle all your pre-retirement goals — for example, working part-time, kids' schooling, beach house — then you should be considering additional contributions to Super. If you've maxed out super contributions, then go back to Investment and go bananas! This is where true legacy starts to build and you're creating long-term, intergenerational wealth. For many, this is part of their definition of 'Beyond Sufficient'.

Most of our clients have at least $500 to $1000 per month to deploy, as they're not spending it all, and have a few 'options' in terms of how to utilise this extra cash. This is a key reason why they seek financial advice.

At least for us at Sufficient Funds, financial advice is not only about investment returns, although these are important; it is also about everything else in your life, and how you align your money decisions with your desired life. Our goal is to ensure you have the best chance of squeezing every bit of fun, joy, experience, love, happiness and fulfilment you possibly can out of the time you have left. Money is no more than a facilitator for this.

You'll find more in chapter 5 about how and why financial advice might be super valuable to you right now. For now, hopefully you're on your way to DIYing a lot of this, so let's keep pumping!

---

**Note:** Before you take this step make sure you understand that this is general rather than personal advice. What works for one person might not work for you for a bunch of reasons. Please don't act without seeking professional advice.

---

# Goal-focused investment for the win!

Link your investments back to your goals and your definition of Sufficient Funds. At the core of this book, my goal is to help you make the connection between money and life. When you get this right, achieving Sufficient Funds is just around the corner. Aside from aligning your day-to-day spending with your values, and not burning cash on crap you don't care about (tick!), the next time this concept becomes invaluable, and something you cannot skip over, is when you're ready to begin investing.

Investing without a plan is like starting a road trip without checking if the car is roadworthy. You'll enjoy the ride, until you're stuck in the bottom of Death Valley, California in 52 degrees Celsius, squatting among the scorpions in the cacti, dealing with a bad burrito.

You need to know what you want to achieve (chapter 1), and your investment choices need to link back to these specific goals. That's how you'll make sure your investment strategy stands the test of time and doesn't fall apart when the markets momentarily tank, or other external events intervene.

So what kind of plan should you have? It should be specific to your goals and flexible enough to account for the unknowns that life throws at you. For example, let's say your goal is to save up for a house deposit. In that case, your investment strategy should be tailored towards that specific goal. You might be tempted to invest in the share market, thinking it'll give you higher returns than other types of investments. But before you go down that path, ask yourself if it's the best investment strategy for *your goal.*

The share market is volatile, and it can be risky. If you invest there, you need to be prepared to weather the ups and downs, and generally this means having time on your side (usually at least five to seven years). If you're saving up for a house deposit and you're on track for achieving this sooner than, say, three years, you might not have the luxury of waiting for the markets to recover.

So you need to think about your investment strategy in a different way. You might consider investing in a high-interest savings account or term deposit, which will provide a lower-risk way to grow your money. In Australia, you could also consider the First Home Super Saver Scheme as a tax-effective option to build wealth, without the same risk as the share market, as well as some great tax benefits that will further enhance your return.

But let's say your goal is different. Along with many of our clients, you might want to create a financial freedom fund that allows you to reduce your work hours when you hit 45 years old to work on your side-hustle, spend more time with the family or take extended breaks to explore the world. In that case, your investment strategy will be different. You might need to consider a mix of investments that provide both growth and income to fund your lifestyle.

Or perhaps you're funding private schooling for your kids (chapter 4). Private education can be expensive, so it's important to start planning and investing early. You could consider education bonds or investment accounts that offer tax benefits and are specifically designed for education expenses.

But here's the thing: life changes. We all know that, and these days the rate of change is a lot faster than it was for our parents. You might set a goal today and find that in a year's time your circumstances have completely flipped. Maybe you've had a phenomenal business opportunity, found a new partner or decided to start a family. That's why your investment strategy needs to be fluid and flexible enough to account for the guaranteed unknowns that life throws at us.

Let's say you've been diligently saving for a deposit on a house, but then you're offered a dream job opportunity in New York and you have to drop everything. We work with a lot of junior doctors who find themselves in this sort of situation. To maximise your career prospects early, the ability to be flexible around where you're living may be crucial. Tash and I have moved cities three times for different reasons. The first two were career-focused moves that paid off big time. When this happens your investment strategy may need to change. You may need to adjust your savings goals or put your money into investments that can be accessed quickly (access to an investment is known as liquidity).

Or let's say you've been building up your financial freedom fund, but then face unexpected medical bills over and above your emergency fund (chapter 2), so you need to dip into those savings to cover the costs. Your investment strategy needs to be flexible enough to accommodate these changes then allow you to rebuild your emergency fund without derailing your long-term goals.

Whether you're saving for a home deposit, funding private schooling for your kids or creating a financial freedom fund, being able to make this clear link to your goals ensures you stay motivated and removes the emotion from investing, and when you hit the inevitable potholes you are prepared, not stressed, and can adjust as you go.

The bottom line is this: investing without a plan is like driving around a new city without your map app. Sure, you might stumble on hidden treasures, but more likely you'll end up lost and frustrated. When it comes to money, this is not cool and is the opposite of what I want for you. This is how to make sure your investment strategy stands the test of time and helps you achieve the life you want to live.

# Debunking the tax myth

We all love our tax deductions, right! 'I'm paying too much tax — how do I reduce it?' I have this conversation with my clients all the time. Sadly, there's a myth when it comes to tax deductions that not everyone is aware of.

There are lots of opportunities out there that, for better or worse, offer tax deductions as a 'benefit'. We often see these tax deductions mistakenly being used as *the* reason for making a significant financial decision. This might be for an investment, a business trip, a novated car lease package through work, a donation, personal insurance or some other form of spending.

Let's get one thing clear. When you get tax back through your tax return, it's because you've already spent the money … *and* you only get a portion of it back.

If you were already going to spend this money, then go bananas and find every legal loophole to get that tax back. However, if you're yet to spend (to invest, donate or lease that car) and are weighing up your options, you need to pause and make sure you're acting for the right reasons.

Table 3.1 (overleaf) shows the 2024/25 personal tax thresholds in Australia.

**Table 3.1: 2024/25 personal tax thresholds in Australia\***

| Taxable income | Tax on this income |
|---|---|
| 0 – $18 200 | Nil |
| $18 200 – $45 000 | 16% |
| $45 001 – $135 000 | 30% |
| $135 001 – $190 000 | 37% |
| $190 001 and over | 45% |

\* To avoid confusion I've omitted the Medicare levy of 2 per cent. Including this levy you pay 2 cents' additional tax per $1 earned at each rate—for example, 37c becomes 39c tax if you earn between $135 001 and $190 000.

Source: © Commonwealth of Australia

So if you earn $145 000, the $10 000 you earn above $135 000 is taxed at 37 per cent. Therefore, on a tax-deductible donation of $10, you will receive 37 cents per $1, or $3.70 back when you do your tax return. Effectively, you've lost (or in this case donated) $6.30.

The tax-deduction conversation can sometimes go something like this:

*Investor chasing gold at the end of mythical tax rainbow:* 'Guess what! I'm buying an investment property, and it's tax deductible!'

*Concerned friend:* 'Great! Where is it? Is it going to grow in value and give you a good rental return?'

*Investor:* 'Dunno, but I'll get a better tax return each year!'

What they're really saying is: 'Guess what! I'm going to drop a dollar. But it's okay, because I still get to pick up 37 cents!'

Not. Cool.

A tax deduction can help make an investment more affordable, but if that investment doesn't perform, you still lose.

I see this with new clients all the time. Many of us have fallen into the trap of using the idea of a tax deduction as an excuse for purchasing something. It's like a discount in a way. The trouble is, this type of behaviour will lead you into a false sense of security, feeling like you have your finances under control. And that feeling is dangerous if it leads you to make decisions based on false assumptions like this.

Stop and ask yourself whether you're really benefiting. If you're not sure, speak to a professional.

Let me shout this out one more time: if you're tempted to do something purely for the tax deduction, please don't.

Investing, purchasing insurance, leasing a car or making any other decision that involves spending to get a tax deduction? Do it because it's a good idea that you would have done without the tax benefit, and now you can claim that spending back as a bonus.

I hope this helps clear up this myth and ensure you think twice about chasing tax breaks that might not be all that helpful for you. Remember that when you have a large amount of tax to pay, this can only ever come about because you've made good money. I'm not saying don't go hard trying to legally retrieve as much of this as possible, but do it with options that are still beneficial.

# Tax effectiveness—before you invest you need this...

Let's dive deeper into investing and taxes in Australia. As you strive for Sufficient Funds, choosing the right tax structure is key. In fact, for many investors, getting this one step right can have a far more significant impact on the benefit of investing than whether your shares, property or otherwise generates a 1, 5 or 10 per cent return! Let me break it down for you.

We all know that taxes can take a big bite out of any income we make. This is true of investment returns too. If you're not paying attention to tax when you choose your investments, you could be leaving a heap of cash on the table. For example, investing in superannuation can be a tax-effective strategy for long-term savings. Imagine you're investing $10 000 a year for 30 years. If your gross (pre-tax) investment annual return is 8.5 per cent and you invest that money in your own name at a 30 per cent tax rate, you'll end up with around $885 000 after 30 years. However, if you invest that same amount in a 15 per cent tax environment such as superannuation, you'll end up with around $1.13 million. That's a difference of $245 000 just because you chose a more tax-effective strategy!

The rule to remember: get your tax structure right upfront! It can be super costly to make changes down the line. For example, a transfer of ownership of an investment property or shares from you to a spouse would be seen as a sale, and you would need to pay capital gains tax (CGT) on any gains made on the investment at the time of 'sale'. Your spouse would need to pay stamp duty to the relevant state revenue office for the portion of the property they are purchasing. This is why it makes sense to do your homework or seek professional advice upfront to avoid a potentially costly tax error!

There are several different tax structures available, each with its own pros and cons. Let's take a closer look.

## 1. Investing in your own name

First up, investing in your own name is the simplest option. Any income or capital gains generated from your investments will be taxed at your individual tax rate. This option is ideal if you're just starting out, but if you're a high-income earner, this can result in a significant tax burden. For example, from the 2024/25 tax year onwards, if you earn over $190 000 a year, you'll be subject to the top marginal tax rate of 45 per cent. This means any income or capital gains you generate from your investments will be taxed at this rate.

## 2. Investment bonds (or insurance bonds)

Investment bonds, a lesser-known product but widely used by those in the know, are similar to superannuation in that withdrawals become tax-free after a certain point, usually 10 years, but differ from super in that you don't have to be retired to cash in. This can make investment bonds a great option if you're saving for the long term but don't want to be restricted by the rules of super or you have already maxed out your concessional (pre-tax) contributions to super.

Investment bonds pay tax on your behalf at a maximum of the company tax rate of 30 per cent. However, some products specifically apply an approach where they can significantly reduce this rate, and this approach alone can make it incredibly attractive for many investors.

Be aware that because of the tax benefits available, there are also a few rules around how much you can contribute (usually only 125 per cent of last year's contribution) and the 10-year access point for tax-free withdrawals.

Some of these products are widely used for saving for children's education. There can be additional tax benefits if used specifically for education, and a number of our clients utilise this special structure where appropriate.

## 3. Family trusts

A family trust is a legal structure where assets are held and managed by a trustee for its beneficiaries. This option can be great if you want to invest with your family or distribute income to those in a lower tax bracket. The trust's income is usually distributed to beneficiaries based on their individual tax rates. This means that if you have family members who earn less than you, you may be able to distribute the income generated from your investments to them, thereby reducing your overall tax liability. Note this is a strategy that should only ever be acted upon as a result of good financial advice.

There are some downsides to using a family trust, however. One of the main ones is the cost of setting it up and maintaining it. You'll need to engage a lawyer or an accountant to set up the trust, and you'll need to pay annual fees to maintain it. And it becomes another entity for which you are responsible when it comes to reporting to the ATO. Additionally, there are some restrictions on the types of investments you can make through a family trust.

# 4. Using a company

Investing through a company is another option to consider. This structure can provide tax benefits, as the company tax rate is generally lower than the individual tax rate. The current company tax rate in Australia is either 25 per cent or 30 per cent, depending on turnover and the percentage of total income for the company that is passive income (significantly lower than the top individual tax rate of 45 per cent). This means that if you invest through a company, any income or capital gains generated from your investments will be taxed at this lower rate.

However, there are some downsides to using a company. Setting up and running a company can be costly and time-consuming. You'll need to register your company with the Australian Securities and Investments Commission (ASIC), and you'll need to comply with a range of legal and regulatory requirements. A company is also not able to claim what is known as the capital gains tax discount. This 50 per cent discount applies to assets personally owned, but not company owned, whereby you can claim a 50 per cent discount for any asset you sell for a gain, as long as the asset was held for longer than 12 months.

# 5. Superannuation

A lot of people see super as an investment, rather than as a tax structure. Please understand that a tax structure is all it is. You choose your investments within super, but it is not itself an 'investment'.

Super is how we all save for retirement and is one of the most tax-effective ways to stack your funds for the long term. Contributions to super can be made concessionally (pre-tax), helping you to minimise tax on the way in, and investment earnings inside super are also taxed at a lower rate.

The major limitation to super is accessibility. Generally, you won't be able to access your super until you reach preservation age, which for most readers of this book will be 60, and after you have stopped work. Additionally, there are limits on the amount of money you can contribute to superannuation each year.

# Investment—your third stack of Sufficient Funds

Mad stacks sitting idle are better than no stacks at all. What's even better are mad stacks multiplying themselves over time. This is your third stack of Sufficient Funds: Investment. Let's look at your options.

## The share market

Purchasing shares — otherwise known as equities or stocks — makes you a part owner of a business. They can be a very good long-term investment. They can also be traded fairly quickly if you need access to your funds. You can benefit from future increases in share price as well as from possible income in the form of dividends when the company distributes any profits.

You can purchase shares directly via an online broker. Broker options include bank-owned firms like CommSec and nabtrade that historically have been more expensive, or other competitors in the market that are offering very low or no fees, like Pearler, Selfwealth or Sharesies. All these brokers give you the flexibility and control to buy and sell shares at will.

Alternatively, you can purchase via a more traditional human stockbroker, where you'll generally pay a lot more per transaction but also for the advice that comes with it.

You can also invest in share markets by using a range of different structures that you may have heard of, the most common being managed funds and exchange-traded funds (ETFs).

Here, I'll outline some more information on some of the more popular options for investing in shares, including why these may or may not be right for you:

## Micro-investing

These mobile apps allow you to invest small amounts of money (as little as 1 cent in some cases) into various investment options, such as ETFs or individual stocks. The apps typically charge low fees and can help people get started with investing even if they don't have a lot of money to spare.

There are numerous apps out there, and a simple search of 'micro investing' in the app store will bring these up. Be sure to do your due diligence to determine that whichever app you choose to invest through is backed by an Australian company with an AFSL (Australian Financial Services Licence). This means they are regulated by ASIC and are required to protect your personal info. Checking out the developer's privacy policy is also key.

Benefits of micro-investing include:

- *Ease of use.* First and foremost, these apps are easy to get started with a simple download and registration, and they remain easy to use for regular, hassle-free investing, accessible on your phone. For most of us who are time-poor, the ability to take a quick squiz and toggle through your investments while sitting on the train, whiling away time in a waiting room or waiting for kids' sport to finally wrap up, this is a smart choice.

- *Low barrier to entry.* Most apps allow users to start investing with very small amounts of money, making it super simple to build up a diversified portfolio over time. Some apps even allow 'round-ups', where you can round your everyday purchases up and use your spare change to invest. Some have kids' investing options, which can make the concept of investing on behalf of your kids an easy win. Parent-managed kids' portfolios are also a great way to introduce young children to the concept of investing (more than we ever learned in school!).

- *Set and forget.* Many micro-investing apps allow you to set up effortless, automatic deposits directly from your savings. Automation, similar to what I discussed around your savings, can save on brainpower, especially if your mental load is already stacked against you, or if you're tempted to use your loose change somewhere else.

Potential watchouts include:

- *Fees can add up.* Most of these apps operate with monthly fees, which are subject to future increases. These need to be taken into account when you look at the overall value of your investment. If you have an account set up, but aren't using it, the monthly fees may still be deducted.

- *Fewer options, less control.* Not every share is available. Micro-investing apps may offer a limited selection of investment options, which may not suit you, particularly if you're an experienced investor or have a specific desire to stick to or avoid certain types of shares for ethical reasons. Your investment carries the same risks as all other share investments. The share market has safer and more volatile shares. You choose your risk tolerance, but you don't get to choose specific shares.

- *Cool your swipe finger.* It's an app, not a game. In an increasingly gamified world, having access to your share investments with the swipe of your phone screen may benefit some, but is a risk if you forget you're playing with real funds, especially if you see quick wins!

## Exchange-traded funds (ETFs)

Think of ETFs as a way to pool your stacks so you have more buying power, like chipping in with mates for holiday accommodation. You can afford a more expensive place to stay and enjoy the benefits that this brings, like access to more facilities or a better location.

ETFs pool together funds from many investors to purchase a mix of shares, bonds or other assets. As the name suggests, they are traded on stock exchanges like individual stocks, and as such they allow huge instant diversification across a range of asset classes. Buying on a stock exchange means you use a stockbroker as described above, and pay a fee (known as brokerage) for each purchase.

Benefits of investing in ETFs include:

- *Flexibility.* You can buy and sell ETFs in the same way as you would shares in an individual company.

- *Diversify your portfolio.* Achieving a higher rate of diversification with ETFs than you would with direct shares is just one of the advantages. ETFs enable diversification across a wide range of asset classes (think cash, shares, property, infrastructure), as well as regions (go global!) and sectors.

Pitfalls that you'll need to watch out for with ETFs include:

- *Risk is real.* Although your investment may be more diversified in an ETF than with single share picks, market risk can be just as high. Again, take this volatility into account and make sure you can afford the impact to your overall investments should markets fall steeply.

- *This isn't 'choose your own adventure'.* You won't have as much choice or control of the underlying assets that make up an ETF as you would with direct shares, where you are selecting exactly what companies to invest in. As with micro-investing apps, this lack of control may not suit the more experienced investor or those with specific preferences.

- *Yep, fees again.* Fees for ETFs may be lower than some managed funds, for example, but they still exist and you'll need to take them into account. You'll also need to weigh up whether the reduced admin cost is worth sacrificing the service and expertise that comes with a managed fund.

## Managed funds

Similar to ETFs, managed funds (mutual funds in America) combine money from multiple investors to enable greater buying power. With managed funds the investment is used to purchase a portfolio of assets, which can include a combination of shares, bonds, property and/or cash. As the name suggests, the fund is then managed by a professional fund manager.

Managed funds are accessed either directly by applying to a particular fund online via their Product Disclosure Statement (PDS) or alternatively through a platform. This is a very handy tool commonly utilised by financial advisers. A platform, also known as a wrap account, comes with a fee, so this needs to be weighed up against the cost of using a broker if purchasing similar ETFs, as previously described. The winner will generally depend on how much and how regularly you are planning to invest, as well as how many different funds you're considering investing in. A platform generally offers far superior reporting, including tax reporting, which can be a huge time saver for you as well as a cost saver when it comes to how much your accountant needs to charge you to bring it all together!

Benefits of investing in managed funds include:

- *Regular investment is often cheaper and easier.* With ETFs you pay brokerage for each trade so it may be suitable for larger or irregular investment. There are changes coming in this space so it is improving. The managed fund version of the investment can work out cheaper than the ETF version if you want to automate a regular, perhaps monthly contribution towards your investments. As discussed in chapter 2, automation leads to flow. When it comes to investment, it also ensures you're not second guessing when to invest, as this is a fool's game and leads you away from the goal of keeping it simple so you can focus on your strengths. If you invest regularly, set it up automatically and touch it only if your strategy changes, not because you heard the market was going to tank, or otherwise.

- *Leave it to the pros.* Managed funds, like ETFs, come with one solid benefit that can make a big difference to your peace of mind: they are professionally managed by investment experts. No guesswork at your end, which could save you time and brainpower once you've selected your fund(s). This may or may not lead to better returns, but it definitely reduces the decision making. If you're prone to procrastination or second guessing, or you're just generally a more nervous investor, this could be a good fit for you.

- *Diversification.* Like ETFs, managed funds offer you the ability to stack your cash in a variety of assets, and this may reduce your investment risk overall. Although the mix of individual shares or other assets within a managed fund may not be free for the choosing, you may be able to make a higher-level decision around the type of mix you choose, such as Growth (generally a higher proportion of higher-risk, higher-reward assets such as shares and property); Conservative (a reduced amount of risk, with typically more investment in cash or with fixed interest); or Balanced (as the name suggests, a bit of both).

- *Increased access.* If the idea of entering a foreign share market sounds a little out of your league, you're not alone. You might baulk at the idea of investing outside of Australia, but with the instantaneous flow of information now available it's actually riskier *not* to explore beyond our shores. The Australian share market makes up a very small percentage (less than 3 per cent) of the total combined size of global markets and is dominated by a limited number of sectors, for example, resources and finance. A great way to access these markets is through a managed fund. With experienced fund managers who often focus solely on their small piece of the world, you are lowering your risk and can benefit from these harder-to-reach opportunities without having to be an independent expert.

This all sounds like an easy option, but there are some drawbacks:

- *The pros aren't giving it away.* Okay, so professionals don't work for free. Fair enough. The fee you pay comes down to the approach taken by the fund you invest in.

# A note on 'passive' v 'active' funds

In simple terms, your options are either 'active' or 'passive'. Passive investment is where the fund you choose takes an equal stake in every company listed on a particular index. An index is essentially the entire market, or at least a large proportion of it. An example of an index in Australia that you might be familiar with is the ASX200, which is the top 200 stocks by size on the Australian Stock Exchange.

You could choose to take a different approach to investing on the ASX. For instance, you might choose an active fund that holds only, say, 30 to 40 of the stocks available in the ASX200. This fund is going to charge more than the passive fund as there is more work involved. The aim of the active fund is to beat the market, rather than simply riding with the entire market. ETFs and managed funds are similar in that you can choose either active or passive options. Your decision will be based on whether you prefer a low-cost approach, or you believe that by paying a bit more you might be able to make more as well.

- *Jesus, take the wheel.* You're not going to have the same level of control with a managed fund as you could with other types of investment. Don't expect to be calling up your fund manager and reading your shopping list of demands after doing your own research. This is *not* how it works. You sign over your ability to make those micro-decisions when you jump into a managed fund, with your only real decisions being whether to stay or go (that is, should you continue your investment or remove your funds).

- *Complex and inflexible tax.* Managed funds operate as
  trusts and investors in managed funds are unit holders in
  the trust. The tax structuring in this space can be complex,
  but you also have no say in when assets are sold, which
  means capital gains can be triggered at a time you don't
  want them to be. This isn't a non-starter by any means,
  but it's good to understand before you dive in. The same
  applies to ETFs.

## Direct shares

When investors purchase shares of a particular company via a
broker, either online or using a stockbroker as described earlier,
they are purchasing 'direct shares'.

As the investor, you should have at least some general knowledge
of the company, be it a well-known Australian company or one you
have been following. Shares have the potential to offer high returns,
but by investing in a single company you are depending on the
performance of that company.

If you know the company you want to invest in and have done your
research into its past performance and share forecasts from various
reputable commentators, you may be well equipped to jump into a
direct share investment. However, shares can fluctuate significantly
and, unlike with a managed fund, you don't have professionals
watching your assets and making educated decisions.

Benefits of investing in direct shares include:

- *The stakes are high.* There's a reason why movie thrillers
  have been made about stock trading and Wall Street. With

the high stakes comes the potential for massive returns from well-performing companies, and with that comes adrenaline, excitement and superyachts!

• *Welcome to the driver's seat.* Direct investment in shares allows you to have ultimate control over which shares, how many, and when to buy, sell and hold. Another benefit is a small step towards more influence over outcomes as a shareholder, where although you don't have a seat at the boardroom table, you may be invited to shareholder meetings and have the right to vote on certain company decisions.

• *A little somethin' somethin'.* Dividends! A dividend is where the company profits are shared with you, the shareholder. Companies usually pay dividends once or twice a year and, as I described earlier, this income adds to the growth in value to give your total return on investment. This can be a great strategy for building up an ongoing regular source of income over time. Many companies pay dividends to shareholders, which over time and after years of consistent investment can build to provide enough to supplement your income to the extent that you can start to make those work/life shifts to align with your definition of Sufficient Funds. (Note that ETFs and managed funds also have an income component, which is a proportion of the combined value of all dividends paid by the companies held within those funds.) Generally speaking, shares are likely to provide a higher percentage of income after tax and expenses than your regular residential property will, and for many people nearing retirement who have accumulated a lot of property, shares now become a far more attractive vehicle to rely on for ongoing income when employment ceases.

Keep your eyes wide open when dabbling on Wall Street:

- *Be aware of the risk.* You might find you have all your eggs in one basket. The performance of one company can hugely impact your investment, especially if you're not spread across a number of industries. As a result, direct share ownership can carry a higher risk than managed funds or ETFs. With high stakes can come equally dramatic nose dives.

- *Google investment school might not cut it.* Investing in individual stocks can be complex and requires a certain level of knowledge and skill. While you don't need a university degree to be able to understand the basics of the share market, it pays to have good industry knowledge and, even better, good business knowledge in the sector in which you wish to invest. This improves your chances of making sound decisions about the viability of a company before plunging your hard-earned stacks into it. If this is definitely not your forte, you may be better off sticking with an investment option where you have experts making these decisions on your behalf.

## Property

Investment property is everyone's favourite asset class, right? Property is a wonderful vehicle for long-term capital growth. One of the benefits but also the risks is that you're generally borrowing (money nerd talk: borrowing to invest is known as gearing), which means that with lending you're accessing a larger asset than you could otherwise afford to purchase.

Gearing or leveraging into an asset like property means your gains, but also any losses, are amplified. So in theory you can make a lot more over the long term out of doing it in this way, but again it's still a 'growth' asset, which means it still comes with similar risks, and despite a lot of Aussies feeling like it's safer than shares, over the long term they have actually performed very similarly.

So is it still the favourite asset class? Well, it's a tough call these days. There are so many good ways to build wealth that don't take such a huge initial outlay. So for most young people, it's certainly not often their first personal investment purchase, as it used to be.

Property is a lumpy asset (that is, while you can sell a small portion of your share portfolio, with property you can't just cut off the living room and sell it if you need access to cash). It also comes with responsibilities, which can be a hassle.

However, we wouldn't be where we are without some very fortunate growth in property values since we purchased our first home in 2009. Property investment is still a viable option for anyone looking to grow long-term wealth.

But first, unless you're buying in Woop Woop, you'll need to borrow money to invest in property. So just making the purchase is the first hurdle you need to overcome.

In its simplest form, the lender (bank, credit union or building society) will look at two different numbers to work out whether they're happy to lend you the money:

1. *Your affordability.* They will consider your income and expenses to judge whether you'll be able to make the loan repayments each month.

2. *Your equity (basically, the size of your deposit).* At the moment in Australia you need at least a 5 per cent deposit, but it's generally recommended that you have more. You also need to be able to cover stamp duty and your own legal fees to have a solicitor review the contract.

If you already own your own home, you may be able to use the equity (value minus loan amount) in it to draw a larger deposit.

You may be able to use a family member to 'guarantee' some of your property loan if you don't have the minimum deposit and they put their home up to help you out. Speak to your mortgage broker to help you with this.

A good mortgage broker can help you find the most appropriate loan, often at a lower rate than offered to the general public, and will do all the hard yards from application to settlement for you.

Mortgage brokers receive a commission on settlement, once all of the work is done. This is paid by the lender themselves out of their own profit margin, so it doesn't cost you a cent. On top of this they can offer their expert advice, complete all the loan paperwork and negotiate with the lenders so you get exactly what you need.

Generally, a mortgage broker will have access to many lenders. Our team has nearly 50 lenders on their panel. They can shop around all the big banks, but also access those lower-tier and specialist lenders if this is helpful. You'll receive a comparison, generally of three of the most suitable lenders and loan products, and you can then make a decision on who you feel most comfortable with.

Just as with a financial adviser, you'll want a mortgage broker who listens to you, who you feel comfortable working with and who answers all of your questions in a way that makes sense to you. If you're ever made to feel dumb, this is their problem not yours. There are plenty available, so keep on moving until you find a good fit for you!

Here are a few benefits to help determine if an investment property is right for you:

- *If you can't beat inflation, join it.* If there is one risk guaranteed to eat into the value of your hard-earned dollars, it's the increasing cost of living. The good news is that the Australian property market generally rises with inflation. So, while you can't do much about the rising cost of a coldie (I was stung $18.50 for a pint last week!), there's a decent chance your big chunky assets are also increasing in value at least at the rate of everything else around you.

- *Capital gains... ca-ching!* The most obvious reason to invest in property is to benefit from long-term growth in the property market. Australian residential property increased by 382 per cent over the 30 years to 2022, which is an annual average of 5.4 per cent. So if you add rental income, you'll see how property rivals shares for total returns (growth plus income) over the long term.

- *Did someone say tax breaks?* An investment property can attract a range of tax benefits, including deductions for interest on your mortgage, property management fees and maintenance expenses. All of these combined can make it more affordable to hold for the long term. However, *never invest in something, or make any financial decision for that matter, just for the tax benefits! If it's not growing, providing a strong income, or both, it's not working!*

- *It exists IRL! Property is a tangible asset.* Unlike stocks and shares, you can see it, feel it, walk through it, make a video and post it to socials ... If you want to be able to see your investment with your own eyes, property may be right for you. The catch here is to not allow emotion to enter your investment decisions. Just like investing in shares, this is about the numbers (growth, income, tax benefits), not about what it looks like and whether the tenant forgets to mow the lawn!

- *Status (ew, did I really just say that?).* Yep, reflecting back on your definition of Sufficient, having something to show for your hard-earned cash, and if you're a closet 'keeping up with the Joneses' type, an investment property might just satisfy your deepest inclinations. If joining the ranks of property owners gives you a sense of accomplishment and pride, and it makes sense financially, then get stuck in!

- *Rental income.* If you're over the idea of lining someone else's pocket in the rental market, switching up the stakes and being the landlord yourself might be an ideal component of your investment portfolio. While building equity in your property you can also collect rental income. This is supplementary income and may be the difference between working that full-time gig or dialling back the hours to spend with family or on a side-hustle.

- *Create a legacy for the next generation.* Property can provide a legacy for the next generation. By owning property, you can pass down an asset that can provide financial security and stability for your loved ones in years to come.

On the flip side, here are a few watchouts you'll want to keep in mind when deciding if investing in property meets your definition of Sufficient:

- *You're playing the long game.* This means having patience. You'll need to be prepared to hold onto your property asset for a number of years to see the potential benefits. Property isn't a liquid asset (you can't get your cash out unless you sell the whole thing), and it requires significant costs to buy (stamp duty and legal fees) and sell (real estate agent's fee). Selling can take time. If you find yourself in a financial situation where you need to sell your property quickly, you may need to accept a lower offer, potentially even lower than what you originally paid. If you're relying on rental income, there's always the potential of a vacancy that impacts cash flow, so be aware that rental does not guarantee a continuous flow of income each month.

- *It's a chunk of cash — like, a lot a lot!* Property in Australia is expensive. You will be committing a significant amount of your hard-earned to get your foot in the door. This can seem hard to reach for singles and even couples. It is not unusual to see parents acting as guarantor on loans for their adult children, and this comes with its own issues. The financial interactions can be complex, not to mention the emotional side of financially relying on parents as an adult.

- *Beware of the competition.* You're not alone in this... if it feels like everyone's doing it, that's because they are! The Australian property market can be highly competitive. Recent years have seen record numbers of people inspecting properties prior to sale and record bids at auction. All this is not for the faint-hearted. When it's an investment property, not your dream home, get your heart out of the game. If you're likely to fall in love with a property and make a dumb move as a result, get someone else to help out. This is where many of our clients work with a buyer's agent.

A buyer's agent (or buyer's advocate) is a licensed real estate agent who, instead of working for the seller, will for a fee work for you. A buyer's agent's service can include coaching and understanding your goals and objectives, completing in-depth research with access to paid data sources, relationships with agents that allow early access to properties or 'off-market' opportunities, and negotiating on your behalf. They will also work closely with your mortgage broker to understand capacity for borrowing, and your financial adviser to align with your overall budget and longer-term life plan. The benefits of this are usually a combination of time and cost saving (net of the fee you pay) as well as avoiding decision fatigue and making a confident purchase. If going it alone, you need to be prepared to do your research, act fast and be strategic to secure the ideal investment property.

- *Climb aboard the rates rollercoaster!* Interest rates can fluctuate quickly, and given most investors are borrowing to make their purchases, this becomes a major part of the cost. The market can be unpredictable as it responds to a range of factors, including government policy and economic conditions. Part of property investing is being along for this ride, but make sure you've played out the scenario if rates rise significantly, and know if you can afford the hike.

- *I'm not high maintenance... but my investment property is!* Unlike less tangible assets, when we're dealing with appliances, walls, roofs and doors, things actually break. And then there are the tenants! You've heard the horror stories, and thankfully this isn't most people's experience, but still worth keeping in mind. The good news is that property managers can take care of almost all repairs and maintenance, as well as managing the tenants, for a fee. Maintenance costs and insurance and property management fees can add up over time, so run your numbers upfront and always ensure you have sufficient buffers in place.

The bottom line is the more research you do, scenarios you envision and time you take to understand the numbers, the wiser your property investment choices will be.

Hit us up at Sufficient Funds Home Loans for expert help in finding the right loan and guidance on whether you have the right amount of money to make this work.

# Crypto

We've all seen the hype around Bitcoin play out over the past decade during the emergence of this alternative currency. Bitcoin launched in 2009 and led the way for other cryptocurrencies, with thousands of cryptos now in existence.

Essentially, crypto is a virtual or digital currency that can be used as a medium of exchange.

It does not require government issue or control, or assistance from financial institutions to process payments. Instead, it uses special encryption techniques to keep data secure, store and create 'monetary units', and verify transactions within a decentralised, digital public ledger (a blockchain).

While there are many cryptos in existence, not all of them are active and most are likely to fail as an investment. This is a highly speculative area and there is a risk that government regulation will play a huge part in its future success or failure. Nevertheless, Bitcoin has created multi-millionaires almost overnight, and in recent years has caused enormous pain for those buying in right before it fell off a cliff.

I believe crypto will continue to grow as a major player in the money world but the risk you take in picking the right one as an investment makes it pretty tough to justify getting into with more than a very small portion of your available cash.

Here's a true story. In 2013 I watched Tim Ferriss' *Random Show* (check out episode 21 at around 36 minutes) and seriously contemplated investing in Bitcoin. I didn't. Today, if you're after an eye-watering Google search, type in 'How much would I have if I had invested $100 in bitcoin in...' and add any year from its birth in 2009. In 2013, $100 would have bought me one Bitcoin, which today (but maybe not tomorrow) would be worth $108 000. Who's counting!

So is it a no-brainer to dabble in crypto? Here are some brief points to consider when determining if cryptocurrency investment makes sense on your path to Sufficient Funds.

Benefits of investing in cryptocurrency may include:

- *Bright shiny objects!* It's still relatively new. It's a novelty. It feels exciting. If this speaks to you, and motivates you to save, then invest wisely, this could be a part of your strategy. Sure, crypto has been around for a while now, but in comparison to traditional investment options, it's still in its infancy. Making the move to invest now could mean you're jumping in on the first floor (the ground floor would have been 2013!), before potential future growth, both in profit and popularity. This is by no means guaranteed, but if you are attracted to things that might go boom, and have a healthy buffer to allow for volatility, it may be worth a crack.

- *Banks are for boomers... join the revolution!* Okay, so crypto is a sure-fire way to break free from the clutches of the traditional banking system. If, like me, you're repelled by the smell of rich mahogany desks and the sight of fabric panel cubicle walls, this is one investment vehicle that doesn't require a visit to a bank or waiting on hold for 45 minutes to speak to a human. Additionally, bank fees and waiting for days for funds to clear are a thing of the past. For the forward thinkers, this digital asset is a revolutionary way of investing and thinking about money.

- *Self-serve.* Crypto is bought and sold online where you can make direct transactions without the need for any intermediaries. You're in charge of your own funds and how to use them. With no bank involvement, and currently without much government intervention, there's no overarching authority telling you what you can and can't do with your funds.

- *Embrace tech.* This investment type is as modern as it gets. We are on a tech exponential curve where understanding and embracing tech is really the only option for future generations. Our money world has already been upended in recent years, with most of us now getting by day-to-day without cash (remember coins and notes?) in our hands. You already know what it's like not to actually physically see your money, so the leap to digital assets isn't that great. If you're already fairly tech-savvy or have a desire to not be left behind, this type of investment may speak to your values.

- *Again, who doesn't love diversification?* Our old mate Warren Buffett famously said that diversification is for those investors who don't know what they're doing, but that was well and truly pre-crypto, and long before the digital self-service fintech world we now live in. I like to think of diversification of your investment portfolio as being humble enough to admit we don't always have all the answers, especially given the exponential rate of tech advancement. So, as with the other investment types outlined above, not putting all your eggs in one basket is generally a smart move. Spreading your investments across a range of options helps reduce the overall risk should markets drop due to unexpected events (did somebody say worldwide pandemic?).

Given cryptocurrency's relative immaturity, the potential pitfalls need to be weighed up carefully. FOMO is real and just because someone else is investing in crypto doesn't mean you should too. Do your research and make an informed decision.

Here are a few of the more obvious watchouts of investing in cryptocurrency:

- *It's a good ol' fashioned hoe-down!... well kinda.* It has to be stated that some of this is cowboy stuff—it's the wild west! As for anything new, regulations are yet to fully catch up to cryptocurrency investing globally, and with the rate of tech development it may be a game of catchup for quite some time. That said, a new Bill, the Digital Assets (Market Regulation) Bill 2023, was introduced in federal Parliament in March 2023 that, if and when passed, will see Australia's first specific regulations of the crypto market.

  Until then, if something goes wrong, the pathway for any resolution is unclear, so you need to be aware that a volatile market combined with a lack of regulation makes crypto a much riskier investment than traditional options.

- *Tax dodge myth.* Although regulations may be taking a while to catch up, it's a myth that crypto is completely private and untraceable. The ATO is cracking down on crypto income, so declare or beware. Another myth is that earnings from crypto are not taxable. The ATO will view this as income so be very careful if you're cashing in to ensure you speak with your accountant as to how this should be treated.

- *It's not liquid gold.* On the flip side of this asset type being completely digital and able to be accessed using a self-service model, cryptocurrency is not always as liquid as some more traditional assets. If you find yourself in a position where you need to sell off your coins fast to access cash, it can be difficult, as each sale still needs a willing buyer and will depend on the users on the particular exchange you've chosen to use.

- *Nerd alert — you'll need to do your homework.* Okay, the learning curve is real! Be prepared for your brain to hurt a little bit. Cryptocurrency is a whole new world, new language, new financial ecosystem that you need to get your head around. Concepts like wallets, exchanges and blockchain are just the beginning. No wonder Parliament is taking their time ... hehe!

- *Danger is real, but fear is a choice!* Don't panic, but crypto investment is considered risky business and it's not for the faint-hearted. You need to be prepared (mentally and financially) to take the risk. Markets can rise quickly and fall in an instant. Potentially high rewards may require high risks. It can be a bit of a rollercoaster — full of thrills as your investment rises but also nauseatingly steep descents. You may need to hang on through a few ups and downs, so if adrenalin isn't your thing, or you just like your money too damn much, it may be best to stick to the carousel!

Our Bitcoin investment is currently up 24 per cent, but it's been a journey to get to this point. Figure 3.1 shows the price of Bitcoin between when we first invested in November 2021 and now. It began with a very slippery slope downwards and is a good example of why you do not invest with money that you can't afford to lose. This was an investment of stacks that we knew we wouldn't miss at all if it completely disappeared. A good reminder to tread very carefully!

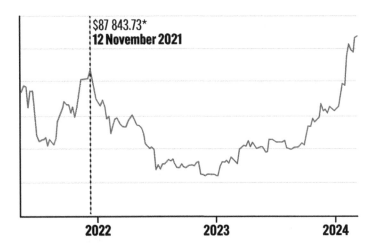

**Figure 3.1: our Bitcoin journey**

\* BTC price in AUD.

Source: Adapted data from CoinMarketCap.com

- *Scams and security.* Scams are highly prevalent in the crypto world. There are unfortunately plenty of opportunities for scammers to take advantage of vulnerable security as well as new players. From fake coin offerings to phishing scams, you need to be on high alert. If your wallet or exchange is hacked, your entire investment could be lost. There is little recourse in an underregulated environment, so keeping your eyes wide open is essential.

So weigh up your risks carefully. If I choose to invest in crypto, I commit only a very small portion of my total investable assets — an absolute maximum of 5 per cent — and also make sure that it's money I won't miss if it disappears overnight.

---

## A final word on investment

As you weigh up your investment options, make sure you keep going back to your drivers—your definition of Sufficient Funds. Remember that you don't just have to choose one. Over time a large portfolio of all asset classes can be the best way to manage risk. Keeping your personal goals in mind and being self-aware of your investment knowledge and your appetite for risk will help you make investment decisions that suit your individual preferences and keep you on track to achieve your Sufficient life.

---

# Superannuation—the fourth stack of Sufficient Funds

Longevity experts are talking about innovations that are really shaking up the way we view old age. Think stem cells to repair heart damage and injections that could prevent Alzheimer's. Although we don't have these yet, think about what your retirement years could look like once some of the more common ailments are reduced or even eradicated in the next decade or so.

# How do you get your own Cayman Islands bank account?

Wouldn't you love to find:

1. a legal source of tax-free income that you never have to report to the ATO

2. a place where you can sell assets that have been growing in value for decades, without capital gains tax?

Well... you know that boring place your parents talk about in relation to their retirement savings? You know it, and I'm here for it! Super is way sexier than you think!

Superannuation takes you as close to that illusive Cayman Islands bank account as you'll probably ever get. For most people, it's their very first investment account, opened in line with their first J.O.B, and when they get started this early, they can pump it consistently for 40+ years!

# The transfer balance cap and why reaching it is a great financial goal

To access your super, you need to hit what's known as preservation age, which for most people is around 60 (as long as you've retired), or 65 if they are still working. Until this time, they accumulate assets in super under — wait for it! — the *Accumulation Phase*. Once they retire, though, most people transfer their entire balance to the *Pension Phase*. There is a tax differential between these two stages. Any earnings and growth of your investments within super drops from being taxed at 15 per cent during accumulation, to 0 per cent when switched to pension. Hello tax haven — where's my pina colada?!

The transfer balance cap is the total amount of super you can transfer into a tax-free pension account. At the time of writing, this limit is $1.9 million per person. This is reviewed annually and increased in line with inflation in $100 000 increments. So if you're a couple who can save enough and you play it right, you can get $3.4 million into this special haven, which could set you up for an incredibly comfortable latter period of your life.

Without a crazy amount of risk and drama this type of combined super balance for a couple would give you a tax-free income of $150 000 to $200 000 every year for the rest of your days. Do it right and you'll still leave a good chunk of it for your inheritance-hungry offspring, or a little extra philanthropy (chapter 5).

Superannuation in Australia is a phenomenal place to start your longer-term savings plans. True, for most of you this feels like the extreme long term, and that's okay. Our clients often wonder whether they're too young to think too much about super. But after recently ticking over to 40 and feeling like it was not *so* long ago that I was still 20 years old and driving around the US selling Insufficient Funds trucker caps, I can tell you it will absolutely sneak up!

There's a difference between focusing all your excess cash from your spending plan (chapter 2) to super, and contributing a small percentage of your income in a tax-effective way.

Be careful not to get too caught up in the chatter that the benefits of super won't be around when you get there. The government needs you to be as self-sufficient in retirement as possible, and this is something they put in place, and made compulsory for employers to contribute to on your behalf, over three decades ago!

Super is a phenomenal way to build a really solid nest egg for when you need it later in life. It's all done in a tax-effective environment, which means when you finally do get to access your super, what you see is what you get. Unlike any other investments you build outside super, which may be taxed fairly heavily when you sell them, this pot of gold is all tax free once you hit the right age.

When it comes to strategy, we are always working with clients on finding the right amount to invest in the super stack. Here's how I'd like you to think about your super. It's not the only place for 'retirement savings', but it could be the cream on top.

Of course, it needs to align with your version of Sufficient Funds, but ideally this includes creating huge future buffers if you have the ability, while neither stretching yourself nor sacrificing life now. With buffers full, ideally your story is not: 'I'll pay the house off by the time I retire, and whatever I can get into super will fund my remaining days.' How about this instead: 'I'm on track to pay the house off before I'm 55, and I'm consistently piling mad stacks for my future financial freedom fund (this allows me to work because I choose to, early retirement, three-month travel stints, volunteering, family time) and I'm maxing out super contributions, which will give me the ultimate freedom once I can tap into this.'

Ideally you are also building assets (read: shares, property and other, as discussed earlier in this chapter) outside of super, and outside of your home, so you have financial security and freedom way before you get too old to enjoy it!

One major benefit of contributing to super is that it is essentially 'forced savings'. Your retirement savings are for retirement and, apart from a few early-access options in very specific circumstances, can't legally be spent earlier.

118

The benefit of forced savings is that the money is allocated to a more profitable place before you can spend it. This is linked to the positive behaviour you will have developed from chapter 2.

## The super gap for women

Superannuation is an important part of financial planning for retirement, but in Australia there is a significant gap between the superannuation balances of men and women. This gap, known as the superannuation gap or the gender super gap, recognises the difference in the average superannuation balances between men and women. According to recent studies, the superannuation gap in Australia is significant, with women retiring with a median superannuation balance of $146 900 compared to $204 107 for men, resulting in a gap of 28 per cent.

There are several reasons for the super gap. Firstly, unfortunately women still tend to earn less than men, which means they have less money to put into their superannuation accounts. Women are also more likely to work part-time or in casual positions, which offer lower wages and fewer benefits, such as superannuation contributions. Additionally, women are more likely to take time off work to care for children or other family members, which can result in a significant reduction in their superannuation contributions.

Another reason for the super gap is that women are more likely to work in industries with lower-paid jobs or in occupations that don't offer the same level of superannuation benefits as other industries.

There's also a systemic issue with the superannuation system in Australia that contributes to the super gap. The current system is based on a model in which employees receive superannuation contributions from their employer, but this system does not account for those who work in part-time or casual positions. This means that women who work in these positions are more likely to miss out on superannuation contributions. The Australian Workplace Gender Equality Agency reports that at every age fewer than 50 per cent of women are in the workforce full time.

In our business over 70 per cent of our client base identify as female, including many singles, and couples where the female is the driving force in seeking advice. As a result, this is a conversation we are encouraging with our clients. There is some very generic advice out there for bridging the super gap, such as consolidating super to avoid unnecessary fees and negotiate higher salaries. Fortunately there are some really great strategies we often employ with clients to help address this gap as individuals. Here are the most common four:

- *Government co-contribution.* Here you are able to make a non-concessional (post-tax) contribution, currently up to $1000, and the government will match this with up to $500 contributed to your super fund. There is a low-income threshold but it can often be employed, especially in times out of the workforce or when working part-time.

- *Spouse contributions.* This works for couples, where the higher earner contributes money into the lower earning partner's super fund, and the higher earner receives a tax offset for this.

- *Contribution splitting.* Again for couples, where the higher earning partner has already made concessional (pre-tax) contributions to their super fund and can then split up to

85 per cent of these into the lower earning partner's fund. This can help to equalise your super balances over time and is particularly beneficial when one partner is working part-time or casually on lesser income. We've employed this option with many clients as part of their Money Action Plan.

- *Carry-forward (or catch-up) contributions.* You will recall Nicola in our client case study was contributing above her concessional contribution cap to pump her super. She was using up some of her 'carry-forward' allowance. The same strategy can apply when looking to bolster one partner's super balance. If you've been working part-time, casually or not at all recently, you'll likely have a significant available limit here as it builds up over five years. So as long as you have the cash available, you can action this if you're single or as a couple. If partnered, it doesn't matter whose bank account it's in or where it came from.

  One common question from couples is, 'If we have spare cash to contribute to super and get a tax benefit for this, why would we put it in my account when I pay less tax?' This is a very valid point. However, what it doesn't take into account is the 'transfer balance cap' I discussed earlier, where if one partner exceeds this and the other doesn't then you end up in an inefficient tax position, post-retirement, in perpetuity. It also doesn't take into account the financial insecurity the lower earning, often female, spouse feels knowing that their partner's balance is going to be so much higher at retirement despite decades of partnership in building this plan together. There is no right or wrong answer here; however, it is an important conversation to have.

# Sufficiently Developed

You now know how to plan for growth and building mad momentum. Specifically:

- You have a good understanding of the four stacks of Sufficient Funds: debts, savings, investments and super.

- You've spent time thinking about which of the four stacks you're currently contributing to (remember, it's likely to be more than one).

- You've completed a pre-investment review of your definition of Sufficient (mostly this was done in chapter 1, but it's absolutely worth recapping before making investment choices).

- You've taken the time to understand how certain tax structures will and won't help your end game and to understand the pros and cons to investing using different entities (such as individual vs family trust).

- You now have a good understanding of the different types of asset classes and the investment opportunities within them, and you have begun to make decisions around where to start stacking your hard-earned.

Congrats! You are now on the way to creating your own mad stacks! This is where true financial freedom begins.

Read on to understand when you may need to defend your stacks from life's ups and downs and how to do it!

# CHAPTER FOUR

# Defend—through life's ups and downs

At Sufficient Funds, we call ourselves optimistic realists. Why? Well, the funny thing about having a plan and life goals is that life can at times be completely unpredictable and totally unplannable. As the American TV writer and producer Barbara Hall once put it, 'The path to our destination is not always a straight one. We go down the wrong road, we get lost, we turn back. Maybe it doesn't matter which road we embark on. Maybe what matters is that we embark.'

Despite our best intentions, life has a way of throwing spanners in the works at the most inconvenient moments. We want you to keep this reality in mind as you build out your life and money plans: shit happens, but it'll be okay.

Not only will you have set up your insanely helpful spending plan (chapter 2) and mapped out where to invest any excess funds (chapter 3), but by the time you're done with this chapter you'll also understand how to safeguard yourself and your family against those bumps and bends in the road. I'll talk about defending your financial position: when to use your safety buffer; how to drop everything when you need to; the importance of perspective; and how to protect yourself against the unplannable with insurance.

Over the years, I've seen endless numbers of clients facing unforeseen difficulties — from a serious medical diagnosis to the loss of a partner in a tragic accident, from being laid off to experiencing a relationship breakdown.

I've also witnessed clients benefitting from unanticipated events: an unexpected inheritance from a distant relative; winning Lotto (IRL!); a redundancy that has been positively life-changing.

Because none of these people anticipated these events, they had to change their plans and rethink goals, adjust timelines for reaching their targets and decide what realities to incorporate into their current situation.

As a lot of our clients are under 40 years old, one common and massive change is the addition of kidlets to the party.

I want to acknowledge that, for a multitude of reasons, having children is not on the path for everyone, but it is something I'm asked to advise on every single week. So I'll dive into the impact a family has on finances and I'll tell you how this has panned out for me personally.

None of this means your definition of Sufficient needs to change, but your plan for achieving it may need some tweaks. We may not be able to predict how and when the spanners will be thrown, but we sure as hell can be prepared to dodge them, or catch them and put them to good use!

# Using your emergency fund — remember it's not your money!

I've already covered the emergency fund, one of the foundations of your Spending Plan. Speaking from personal experience, it feels great to have a buffer tucked away. The kicker is there's a good chance you'll need it one day.

In chapter 2, I talked about the concept of tucking away your emergency fund and never thinking about it again. Imagine it's not yours! Because the reality is that if you're seeing it as something you plan to use for something else, it'll play on your emotions. You built this up and felt more and more secure as it grew. You might feel scared that you're accessing your buffer, disappointed that you've reached a situation where you need it, but remember, as long as you've always viewed this as not your own, as long as it was never allocated to anything else, then — crisis averted!

At this point, you're going to need to return to that key element we spoke about before you even started to define your Sufficient life: your mindset. Again, mindset is everything, but when you're stuck in a rut and having to access emergency funds, your mindset is going to be challenged. It's at moments like these that your crystal-clear focus on your values and your definition of Sufficient are going to be critical. Go back and revisit what it is you truly value and remember this: you're not going to be in this rut forever. The situation is temporary. So use your funds, make these hard-saved dollars work for you now to build the steps up and out of the rut. Then focus on the next step: rebuilding your emergency fund.

Once you've used your emergency fund and things are starting to get back on track, STOP! Remember Cruise Control: Your Spending Plan ensured your excess funds from each pay flowed into all the right places. In chapter 3 I talked about some of this excess potentially going into investments or super or both. If you've depleted your emergency fund, your priority needs to be rebuilding it. Decide what you're going to stop contributing to while you rebuild your buffer.

Maybe you aren't having that big trip this year. Divert your holiday funds to the emergency fund. Perhaps you were saving for your third child but the two you have are more than a handful and you're not ready to commit to Kia Carnival life (just yet anyway). Divert these funds. You can also slow down on your investment contributions, just temporarily, if you absolutely must.

## *Remember: emergency fund filled, then fun.*

Be purposeful. Remember how frickin' relieved you were to have that buffer to call on when you needed it? Let that motivate you to regain that original nice round number you started with.

Finally, congratulate yourself! As difficult as it was to go through, this was made possible by your planning ahead and dealing with a problem independently. Being financially secure is one of the most common objectives we hear our clients talk about day in, day out. Your focus on this has allowed you to deal with your actual emergency, instead of creating a new, and possibly longer-term, financial problem. Cracking effort!

# Adding kids, not zeros

**Full disclosure:** It's important to note that I'm coming at this incredibly sensitive topic as a male. If you spend a bit of time on Reddit, you might be familiar with the acronym AITA: Am I the asshole?

So, I fell asleep while Tash was in labour with our first child. AITA? I like to believe I'm not the only partner who's taken a snooze during such a momentous event, but I do acknowledge the non-childbearing privilege the act represents.

Now, while I'm never going to experience every aspect of the following topics, what I can and will bring to this is deep personal experience in a bunch of areas that include planning a family, fertility issues, supporting my wife through pregnancy, major pregnancy complications and extensive time in hospital, as well as pregnancy loss. I'm a dad to two IVF kids who are now five and six years old. We've had babies in intensive care, and day care and school transitions are now relevant, and of course I've been involved in financial planning around these topics for hundreds of clients of Sufficient Funds over the past five or so years. So while we're here I also want to acknowledge that we've been through some really tough times ourselves through all this, I know this can be an emotional topic for a lot of us, as well as a very costly one. I'm incredibly privileged to work with countless young people in building financial plans around these big moments, and my deep understanding of what people are dealing with is based on my having been through it all myself.

Some spanners are more predictable than others. If you know you want to have kids one day, you at least know this is something to prep for, but in my experience nothing prepares you for the life-changing impact of bringing tiny humans into the world. Enjoying the ride is all part of the experience, as they say.

Adding kids into the mix opens up entirely new realms of goals and also financial needs. From medical costs, time off work, day care and school fees, the list grows rapidly and the financial needs you may have had as an individual or couple change just as fast.

Timing for your family plans might be rough estimates or fairly specific, but I highly recommend your plan be flexible enough to allow for the unpredictable nature of trying to conceive. We definitely knew we wanted kids but we had no idea how hard the process was going to be.

We started trying for kids when we were around 30 years old. It took us about four months to fall pregnant. Easy, right?

Unfortunately not. At the end of a rocky first trimester we received news that our baby would not survive and, devastatingly, we had no option but to terminate.

This was October 2013. Tash was told to take a couple of months to recover and after that it was up to us.

That Christmas we bought mountain bikes, something that had been on our list for a while, and Tash organised a ride around northern Laos to raise funds for Care Australia. We returned in April, fitter than ever and thinking this would be the start of our next and more successful round of trying to conceive. This plan, too, was way off.

Tash was diagnosed with endometriosis in October 2014. She had likely lived with it for many years but like most people with endo, she wasn't diagnosed until she was in her 30s. Her diagnosis came after an appendectomy, when her surgeon discovered advanced deep infiltrative endo.

She needed multiple rounds of surgery to remove adhesions that meant many of her organs were stuck together. The impact of endo on fertility is well known and before we were at last able to welcome our baby girl into the world, we undertook a four-year fertility journey that included IVF, Chinese medicine — even religious charms and voodoo statues.

This journey took a lot out of us not only physically, mentally and emotionally, but also financially. IVF and other surgery costs were not something we had planned for. We needed IVF for both our kids and each round cost us around $10 000. Each round of endo surgery was another $5000. With the endo diagnosis, prior extensive surgery and an IVF baby on board, we opted for a private obstetrician and all the costs that came along with it.

At this point, our finances were less than stable. I had left my corporate job and branched out into my own business. Not only was it taking up a huge amount of my time, but in the early days cash was scarce. We were just keeping our heads above water. We were hugely thankful for our emergency fund but we knew we could have been in a much better position had we been able to predict more of this journey.

So many people who come through our MAP™ process are planning for families either immediately or in the future. We dive into the details and I'm in the fortunate position of being able to relate.

Whether they'd like one or two kids or the whole footy team, we work with them to plan for it. If family history, health issues or sexuality point to the possible need for fertility treatment, we include it in the plan.

Because what will eventuate in this space is, to say the least, unpredictable you need to be confident your emergency fund is ready and that you know how you're going to pivot if the shit hits the fan. The fertility journey and accompanying medical diagnoses can be stressful, but having your money sorted will prove to be a massive stress reliever.

We are so grateful things turned out as they did for us. We have two healthy IVF kids, and while Tash still has ongoing medical costs with endo, we know it's an extra line in our budget and we roll with the punches.

We estimate endo has cost us, on average, around $7500 a year for the past decade or so. This cost doesn't include IVF and other fertility treatments and nor does it take into account lost productivity. Because we know endo will be an ongoing cost for our family, we have our 'endo fund' set aside. A recent Australian study has estimated the average economic burden of endo to be around $20 000 per patient per year. This includes health costs, productivity costs and carer/household costs. This is a mind-blowing amount of money when you consider this condition impacts one in seven people with a uterus.

None of us ever wants to plan for either acute or chronic illness, but it's a fact of life and as optimistic realists we recognise the importance of a broad understanding of potential costs, and a chunky emergency fund to boot!

If endo or other chronic illness is a factor for you and you want relatable financial advice to help wade through funding options and still living your life to the fullest, reach out.

*What will you be dealing with, and how much will it cost?* As with any stage in your life, once you decide to have a family (refer back to chapter 2), you'll need to plan. Depending on your income and budget, think about whether you'll save for this in an extra 'squirrel account: baby fund', or whether you can 'cash flow it' with your ongoing income from parental leave (from work and/ or the government's Parental Leave Pay) or sufficient income from a spouse or partner. I've outlined some of the potential costs below.

It may be easy to chunk this planning into the following stages to help both financially and emotionally, as you think it through:

- trying to conceive

- pregnancy

- birth and setup

- time off / parental leave

- back to work

- child care

- schooling.

# Trying to conceive

For a lot of people, this part is effectively free, and fun!

For others, like Tash and me, getting pregnant entails unexpected costs, and budgeting for these can be very difficult if not impossible.

I'm a money nerd at heart but this is one area where the numbers, as long as you have a rough idea of Sufficient, should not dictate the decision. Starting a family might be the start of the single most fulfilling part of your life!

You'll want to be as well-prepared financially as possible but in the end, unless you're swimming in personal debt and aren't making ends meet, you'll move mountains to make this work. Don't overthink it; just be aware.

## IVF

What we have learned in the course of our experience with fertility treatment is that it is highly individualised. A 'formula' that works for one person or couple might not work for another. As a result, timelines and budgets also fluctuate. In fact, our client demographics vary widely so during our Defining Sufficient sessions and annual check-ins we've discussed and planned financially for all options, including fertility treatments and donor, surrogacy and adoption services. Costs vary for each treatment option, and you may need to call on several. We got lucky and IVF was our ticket to having two kids.

At the time of writing, the out-of-pocket cost for a cycle of IVF at most private fertility clinics is a little over $5000. Medications can cost a further $2000. In some states, pre-fertility screening is rebatable and there are government initiatives to help reduce other costs. For example, since 2021 in New South Wales, eligible patients' out-of-pocket costs for a total cycle at some public clinics can be reduced to just over $1000. Public hospital waiting lists may apply in some states at various times, so keep this in mind. Generally, you'll pay a little more for your first round, and a little less for subsequent rounds, should they be needed. If attempts are unsuccessful and should you have frozen embryos available, the costs of a round are roughly halved.

You may be able to pay for IVF with super. Definitely seek advice before even contemplating going down this path, but in general terms, it is sometimes allowed under the condition of release known as compassionate grounds. You will need to meet strict requirements, including the provision of an invoice from a relevant registered medical professional.

There are also some options around payment plans with fertility providers that may be worth checking out. Of course, nothing like this is ever free, so make sure it makes financial sense for you.

## EGG FREEZING

I see many clients whose plans include having kids one day but not right now. Egg freezing is the process of storing unfertilised eggs for a later date. Frozen eggs can remain viable on ice for many years and the process is becoming increasingly common. At present, Medicare rebates (and some public hospital access) will only cover egg freezing if there is a health risk to fertility such as endometriosis or cancer, so elective egg freezing comes at full cost through private providers.

## SURROGACY

This can be one of the more expensive routes to parenthood because added to the costs of IVF and other treatments are legal fees and counselling. Commercial surrogacy is not legal in Australia, and internationally it comes with a significant fee over and above medical and other costs (potentially $100000 to $150000 or more). While for many people that's going to be completely out of the question, for some it may be worth weighing up. The rules here are incredibly complex. If thinking about this, all parties entering a surrogacy arrangement in Australia should seek advice from an experienced family lawyer.

## ADOPTION

Finally, adoption is another pathway to starting or growing a family. In NSW, for example, it costs around $3000. Inter-country adoption is also possible for Australians, with adoption arrangements in place with 13 countries. Inter-country adoption costs about $10000, not counting extra expenses such as travel and accommodation, citizenship costs and legal fees. Some states have hardship policies to help lower income earners access at least some fee relief.

# Pregnancy

**Note:** If you're planning to deliver at a private hospital and you don't yet have private health cover, you will likely face a 12-month wait on pregnancy claims. You'll struggle to find a policy for which that's not the case, so make sure you have this kind of cover in place before you become pregnant.

Ideally you've got eight months of pregnancy to go by the time you've found out. This is your time to get saving if you haven't already, as while your pregnancy might be close to free, having a baby and setting your home up for their arrival does cost. Keep reading for the estimated costs, but this is your window to get financially prepped.

Whether or not you have any underlying health conditions, you may or may not be able to work as usual while you're pregnant. Keep in mind that there may be some timing challenges as you're calculating anticipated income during these months.

# Birth and setup

Costs range from around $3000 to $10000. Remember, spend on what you value most.

## MEDICAL COSTS

Birthing costs will depend on where you plan to deliver. If you choose a public hospital, and you have Medicare, then out-of-pocket costs are likely to be between $0 and $1500. Because of Tash's medical history, we chose a private hospital and our own OB/GYN, and the out-of-pocket cost for each birth was about $5000. That cost included multiple appointments and tests throughout the pregnancy.

## SETTING UP AT HOME

We received some very wise advice when we got pregnant, and now pass it on to anyone who needs it.

> **Public service announcement:** Most expecting parents have already heard the advice you're about to give them so get permission before you deliver it. Pregnancy is hard enough without the repetitive onslaught of well-meaning tricks and tips!

Initially there are four big items — car seat, cot, change table and pram. Basically, the rest can wait! Table 4.1 indicates a range of costs to plan for, based on your savings.

### Table 4.1: baby setup costs

| Item | Gumtree / second-hand | IKEA / Big W | Baller |
|------|----------------------|--------------|--------|
| Pram | From $0 | $200 | $2500+ |
| Cot | From $0 | $200 | $1500+ |
| Change table | From $0 | $100 | $1000 |
| Car seat | Safety first. Don't skimp here! | $150 | $1000 |

As you can see, the price range for this stuff is huge. I did a quick search and found a car seat selling for $10 687 — I wonder if it self-cleans number 3s? There's also a $61 000 pram if you can spare the coin, but I'm pretty sure your little bundle of joy would prefer their parents read up on intergenerational wealth transfer than be treated to an eight-month spin in the Silver Cross Rose Gold Edition (yes, it's covered in actual gold!). You can go nuts with this stuff.

If you land in the middle of this spending range, as we did, you're up for maybe $3000 for these big items, depending on how you roll. Our $600 pram was so damn good we allocated more to really good car seats for both cars to save time mucking around constantly transferring seats between cars. As you know, time is money.

Finally allow $500 for everything else. Most of which can be done in the first few weeks so don't feel the added pressure to have everything purchased before baby arrives. You will want an excuse to get out and about.

Finally, be ultra-clear on things you would appreciate as gifts and let your family and friends know. You might appreciate a pile of clean towels, bibs and wipes or a baby monitor much more than a singing cactus toy. This is the time to be specific about what you need.

## Time off / parental leave

Current data indicates that 60 per cent of employers in Australia offer approximately three months' fully paid parental leave to mum, and quite a few bigger businesses now offer, if not the same, at least something to partners.

Increasingly, companies are contributing to staff super for some portion of the time spent on parental leave. This goes some way to bridging the very real gender pay gap. If this isn't available in your workplace, start to challenge things a little bit. Find companies who do offer these benefits — ideally, direct competitors — and take it to your management team. Start to campaign. You won't be alone.

For primary caregivers who don't earn 'too much' (less than approximately $168 000 in the previous financial year) the federal government also kicks in 20 weeks of parental leave pay based on the minimum wage of approximately $17 500 before tax. Recent changes have included the ability to look at your household income for the financial year, rather than just the income of the primary carer, so if you personally earn 'too much', as long as your combined income is no more than $350 000, you will still qualify.

The good news is that if you are eligible, you can claim both, so you can claim the work leave as well as the paid leave from the government.

'Dad and Partner Pay' was recently removed and is now combined with parental leave pay (previously 18 weeks) for a total of 20 weeks. This can now be shared fully with the partner, but is always at the discretion of the birth mother or the first adoptive parent.

It's important to remember this is basic assistance. It's paid at minimum wage, which does go up every year with inflation, but it's unfortunately not available to everyone. To be eligible you need to meet the income and work tests.

Another recent change that's been super helpful for a few of our clients is in the flexibility of the parental leave system. You can now take this leave in blocks as short as one day, and you and your partner can spread it out between you, so long as you both qualify, until the child turns two. This might work for someone who is self-employed and needs to keep a business running, or someone who can work from home. So, for example, you could work two to three days a week and take the rest of the week as parental leave.

For those who aren't eligible, you're going to need to take this into your own hands and set up your own savings buffers both for starting a family and for getting back to work.

Finally, it may be worth asking your employer about fertility leave. Although it's not very common yet, there are companies (including ours as a small business!) that are offering additional days of paid leave for fertility treatments. If you find yourself in this situation, asking may just be the nudge your employer needs to make this a reality.

## YOUR BUDGET DURING PARENTAL LEAVE

Most of the birth mums we're working with take six to 12 months off for their first child and the partner anywhere from a week or two up to about three months. It all depends on entitlements and what you can afford. And on your work situation. I've been working remotely, as you know, so fortunately or unfortunately for me, hehe, I was there for every single little drama with both kids as newborns. Jokes aside, I'll cherish forever the time we spent together as a young family and I count myself very lucky we could create the flexibility that allowed this.

Depending on your budget, or more specifically your family's reliance on the income(s) of those taking parental leave, you may need to save an extra amount prior to stopping work to get you through. The quick and easy way to do this is to pull out the budget you've already completed (see figure 4.1, overleaf), 'Save as' a new copy, call it 'Parental Leave' and play around. For the most common example of mum taking 12 months off, replace mum's full income with the employer's paid leave plus the government leave (after tax, remember), make frequency 'yearly' and work out how many pay cycles you'll be working since you'll be off work for the full year. Then scroll down to the bottom to see whether there is a positive or negative result.

If the result is positive, you'll be fine. If not, you can see how much you need to save for the year (or however long you'll be away from work), on top of your birth and setup costs. Remember this is a simple addition of a baby fund to the account structure we discussed in chapter 2.

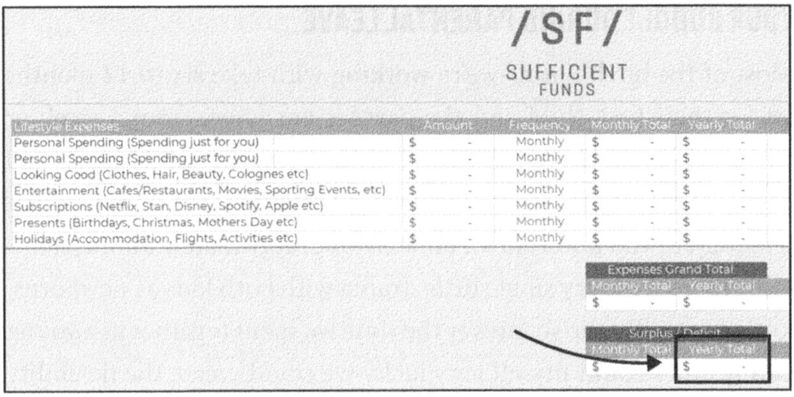

/SF/
SUFFICIENT FUNDS

| Lifestyle Expenses | Amount | Frequency | Monthly Total | Yearly Total |
|---|---|---|---|---|
| Personal Spending (Spending just for you) | $ - | Monthly | $ - | $ - |
| Personal Spending (Spending just for you) | $ - | Monthly | $ - | $ - |
| Looking Good (Clothes, Hair, Beauty, Colognes etc) | $ - | Monthly | $ - | $ - |
| Entertainment (Cafes/Restaurants, Movies, Sporting Events, etc) | $ - | Monthly | $ - | $ - |
| Subscriptions (Netflix, Stan, Disney, Spotify, Apple etc) | $ - | Monthly | $ - | $ - |
| Presents (Birthdays, Christmas, Mothers Day etc) | $ - | Monthly | $ - | $ - |
| Holidays (Accommodation, Flights, Activities etc) | $ - | Monthly | $ - | $ - |

| Expenses Grand Total | |
|---|---|
| Monthly Total | Yearly Total |
| $ - | $ - |

| Surplus / Deficit | |
|---|---|
| Monthly Total | Yearly Total |
| $ | $ - |

**Figure 4.1: parental leave budget**

I've found, both personally and working with many clients, that while babies might reduce our income for a time, they don't usually increase our expenses very much while they're little. Less clubbing and fancy dinners, more nappies and triple-shot flatties — they tend to balance out.

## Back to work

Full-time, part-time, new business or never again? One of the key advantages of achieving Sufficient Funds is doing work you enjoy, so I hope it's not the latter. But for now, let's go with whatever floats your boat.

When you're mapping this out in advance and tossing up between three or four days as an example, plan for three days of income so if you do the extra day, it's a bonus and not a necessity.

My experience is that even the most career-oriented new parents are likely to have a fresh view on work post baby.

Living to your potential and smashing your big work dreams is something I want for everyone, so absolutely keep striving for this, and ideally you will find a balance that works. This goes for partners too. We see lots of partners who, while they may not have shared a lot of the child care early on for financial reasons, balance out to a four-day week or something more flexible once the primary carer is back at work.

Insert day care! At the ripe age of six to 12 months, children are not exactly self-sufficient so being back at work means someone's still got to look after them. If each of you works four days, and if you stagger the days you will be at home, then you only need three days of day care or grandparent support!

Family day care or childcare?

- Family day cares are generally cheaper, smaller operations with fewer kids. They're also likely to offer shorter hours, similar to a school day. They tend to be more flexible than childcare centres, so fees are usually quoted hourly, ranging from about $8 to $18 per hour, with an average of $10.76.

- Childcare (or long day care), as the name suggests, caters more to pre- and post-work hours. Ours is open from 7.00 am to 6.00 pm, which means it's easy to do an early drop off and still get a surf or a ride in before getting stuck into the day! Day rates generally start from about $80 but more commonly are closer to $130 to $180+ before the government subsidy, which, at the time of writing, is 90 per cent for households earning under $80 000, down to 0 per cent for the ballers with a combined income of $530 000 or more.

We lived in Sydney for most of our kids' day care years before, in mid 2021, we moved back to Newcastle, the city where the Insufficient Funds dream had started nearly 20 years earlier! We had no family support in Sydney, so for most of this time both our kids were in day care four days a week.

---

**Pro tip:** If you're expecting a second child, don't plan to pull your older child out of day care while you're juggling a newborn. At this age your child is making lots of little friends and learning hugely valuable social skills, and your 'spare' time is better spent sleeping.

---

Family can also play a huge part here. We've seen it all. Some grandparents seize the opportunity to look after the kids, and others can't get far enough away! Each to their own. There is clearly a financial benefit here. A day a week spent with the grandparents saved us about $10 000 a year. Thanks, Nanna and Pa! This is due to how the subsidies worked while we had two in day care. Thankfully the government has since stepped up to heavily subsidise your second, third and fourth child, if that adventure is calling!

This wraps up this stage of starting a family. The next challenge is probably how to fund the next child or two, should you be planning to grow your family further. There's no doubt this planning is really difficult because there are so many moving pieces and so many unknowns. However, it's an amazing period in your life so please stop, plan and get the money stuff sorted so you can focus on the fun.

## *Schooling*

Unless you're planning to start with private schooling from day one of kindergarten, the transition from day care to school should bring some sweet relief to your bank account!

This is us right now, and so far it's pretty damn good! Six-year-old and five-year-old time is very different from toddler time so, new parents, you've heard it before, but it does get better!

Then there's the extra financial freedom. We dropped from four days a week with two kids at day care to just one, and we saved nearly $18 000 a year. Imagine what you could do with this!

For us, if we chose to take this saving and put it into super or an investment account, we'd have more than $880 000 extra between us by the time we were 60.

Or you might have a $1 million mortgage and choose to pay these savings there instead. This would have you paying out the loan 11 years earlier and save you $290 304 in interest.

You could also seriously dial up the contributions to your travel fund, or like us you could mix it up. What you decide to do is entirely up to you, but this is where you should be crunching the numbers and balancing this with these priorities. The last thing you want is to second guess the decision or be stressing about which way to turn and not realise the significant positive impact each decision can have on the life you're trying to live.

# Private vs public schooling

I've heard every argument under the sun for both sides from people from all extremes of the financial-capability spectrum. This includes speaking at length with people who've sent their kids to private school and acknowledged it probably wasn't necessary or worth the funds, and to others who really couldn't afford it, worked themselves to the bone to make it happen, and don't regret a thing.

I went to public high school in Grafton, where we had two choices, one Catholic, one public. My parents 'offered' to send me to Churchie, a GPS school in Brisbane, for my senior years. I politely declined, as any reserved teenager would when weighing up leaving home, the soccer team and a good crew of friends for boarding school with a bunch of city boys in blazers, more than an hour from a beach.

Grafton schooling, regional and fairly rough, was good for me. I got to interact with kids whose families came from all walks of life. It toughened me up a bit and gave me a grounding in what matters, and this is something I am truly grateful for. Byron Bay's median house price is over $3 000 000 for a number of reasons, and I think one of them is that if heaven exists, it will look a lot like the NSW north coast. It's God's country and will forever occupy a treasured place in my heart.

While not too many people send their kids to private school from kindergarten, it becomes a very real prospect once high school comes around.

You can often find some middle ground, but annual fees for the best of the best range from about $30 000 to $45 000 per child. Add another $25 000+ if boarding.

Let's say that, like my clients Rach and Greg, you live in a city so don't need the boarding option. You have two kids — one is two months old and the other is two — and you plan to spend $30 000 per child per annum, in today's dollars, for their high-school education.

There are three ways to handle this:

1. You have wealthy parents or grandparents who are so insistent on keeping the family tradition alive that they
   · refuse your weak attempts at stopping them pulling out the black AMEX.

2. You earn $400 000+ per annum. You may not have to save in advance: you just cover it with your net income and still live a pretty good life.

3. You start saving or investing as soon as your kids are born and cash in and fund the investment through regular withdrawals from your stacks.

Here's how we did it for Rach and Greg:

- Mapped out each year from today through to the end of school for their youngest to ensure we were as accurate as possible.

- Recommended an investment bond. This product type is very popular for funding longer-term costs like education.

- Started with a $10 000 initial investment, contributing $10 000 in the first year ($833 monthly) and increasing this contribution by 25 per cent each year, through to year 10 and then stopping. This yearly increase aligns with expected increases in income and with other goals, which include paying out the home loan within 10 years.

- You can see in figure 4.2 we made an investment return assumption of 5.95 per cent after tax. The earnings are taxed within the investment bond, which means tax is paid at a lower rate than these guys are expecting to pay personally throughout this time. Bonus!

- This spreadsheet (see figure 4.2) shows how it looked over 20 years.

- You can see withdrawals of $30 000 per annum (plus inflation) for the eldest child begin in year 11. They double two years later, and drop back for the last two years and then, HAPPY DAYS! $26 436 is left over for the 18th-birthday parties and a family trip to Whistler!

My view on this big decision? It depends on the child. Some kids will cruise through the most basic of public schools and their natural talent and focus will see them scoring high results and choosing whatever uni and whatever course they want. Some won't be cut out for any further type of academic pursuit, and this is also fine. You don't need to attend a private school or do a business or science degree to have an incredibly fulfilling career or start an insanely profitable business and make mad stacks if this is what you're seeking.

| Personal Investments | Year 1 | Year 2 | Year 3 | Year 4 | Year 5 | Year 6 | Year 7 | Year 8 | Year 9 | Year 10 | Year 11 |
|---|---|---|---|---|---|---|---|---|---|---|---|
| Inv. Bond #1 (Education) | | | | | | | | | | | |
| Net Earnings: 5.95% pa | | | | | | | | | | | |
| Opening Value | 10,000 | 20,893 | 35,007 | 53,180 | 76,457 | 106,146 | 143,888 | 191,731 | 252,241 | 328,627 | 424,903 |
| Contributions | 10,000 | 12,500 | 15,625 | 19,531 | 24,414 | 30,518 | 38,147 | 47,684 | 59,605 | 74,506 | 0 |
| Earnings | 892 | 1,615 | 2,548 | 3,745 | 5,275 | 7,224 | 9,696 | 12,827 | 16,782 | 21,770 | 23,041 |
| Withdrawals | 0 | 0 | 0 | 0 | 0 | 0 | 0 | 0 | 0 | 0 | 37,660 |
| Closing Value | 20,893 | 35,007 | 53,180 | 76,457 | 106,146 | 143,888 | 191,731 | 252,241 | 328,627 | 424,903 | 410,284 |
| Closing Value (PV) | 20,423 | 33,451 | 49,673 | 69,809 | 94,739 | 125,536 | 163,517 | 210,286 | 267,808 | 338,480 | 319,486 |

| Personal Investments | Year 12 | Year 13 | Year 14 | Year 15 | Year 16 | Year 17 | Year 18 | Year 19 | Year 20 |
|---|---|---|---|---|---|---|---|---|---|
| Inv. Bond #1 (Education) | | | | | | | | | |
| Net Earnings: 5.95% pa | | | | | | | | | |
| Opening Value | 410,284 | 393,877 | 333,799 | 268,225 | 196,784 | 119,083 | 80,435 | 38,435 | 40,722 |
| Contributions | 0 | 0 | 0 | 0 | 0 | 0 | 0 | 0 | 0 |
| Earnings | 22,120 | 18,746 | 15,063 | 11,051 | 6,688 | 4,517 | 2,158 | 2,287 | 2,423 |
| Withdrawals | 38,526 | 78,824 | 80,637 | 82,492 | 84,389 | 43,165 | 44,158 | 0 | 0 |
| Closing Value | 393,877 | 333,799 | 268,225 | 196,784 | 119,083 | 80,435 | 38,435 | 40,722 | 43,145 |
| Closing Value (PV) | 299,815 | 248,372 | 195,093 | 139,912 | 82,764 | 54,646 | 25,525 | 26,436 | 27,379 |

**Figure 4.2: Rach and Greg's investment plan for private school savings**

On the flip side, some kids would absolutely benefit from the extra nurturing, attention and individualised learning that is offered by schools that cost more each month than a $500 000 mortgage. There's a strong argument to be made, too, for the networking kickstart achieved by being connected at this end of the socio-economic spectrum. In the end, make sure it's affordable and focus on what your child needs, not on what you, in line with however many generations before you, believe is right.

> **Note:** This advice is not individualised for you. It was personal advice for Rach and Greg and their special set of circumstances, income, tax and other needs. We created this solution for them after spending a number of hours discussing their personal goals. An education plan by itself isn't worth much; it needs to take into account everything else that's going on. Make sure you seek personal financial advice before investing in this type of product.

# Drop everything

I've already alluded to life's unpredictability. As a financial planner, I pride myself on being able to plan and help predict what lies ahead for my clients, for myself and for my family, but it is really important to note there are some things you simply cannot plan for.

Imagine this for a second (this isn't one for the faint-hearted).

It's just past 5.00 pm on a Friday, a sunny but cold Sydney afternoon, the end of the work week. Tash is 32 weeks pregnant with our son and is just wrapping up at the office and about to head home. Suddenly, and without any prior sign or symptom, she starts bleeding out. When I say bleeding out, we're talking litres. She assumes her waters are breaking, but looks down to see her jeans and white sneakers absolutely soaked with blood.

Super fortunately Tash worked less than 500 metres from Royal North Shore hospital and with maternal instinct in overdrive she decided that driving herself to the hospital with me on the phone would be the quickest way to get help. By the time she pulled up outside emergency, having busted a boom-gate on the way through, there were pools of blood in the car. As she trailed blood through the emergency department, she was met by staff and swiftly moved into a resus bed, where her clothes were cut off and a team of about 15 staff began to gear up.

By the time I got there with Ada, Tash had been prepped for surgery and was about to be wheeled in. The attending OB/GYN made a last-minute decision not to deliver our baby there and then and instead to wait to see how Tash responded to a blood transfusion. Minutes later, she started to crash. The team called a code blue and I was told to leave the room. Mercifully, she bounced straight back and the bleeding finally stopped. The medical notes record she had lost an estimated two litres of blood. Tash spent the next month in hospital as we waited for the next haemorrhage significant enough to make early delivery of the baby necessary. We knew he would be pre-term and we knew at this point there were likely to be complications.

During this month I solo-parented our 16-month-old at home and met Tash at the hospital most days. I had just started Sufficient Funds and I begged forgiveness from our very few clients for work I couldn't deliver on time.

Eden was born by emergency C-section at 35 weeks, but he was a little trouper needing only a feeding tube and a two-week stay in special care. We took him home and enjoyed a week of relative normality. We thought we were in the clear, but it turned out he had contracted a serious infection while he was in special care and he and Tash were taken back to emergency by ambulance. His infection didn't respond to all the antibiotics pumped into his tiny three-week-old premmie body, and we were told he had an antibiotic-resistant strain of bacteria that had entered through his umbilical cord. Again he fought through and was discharged, albeit with a very degraded immune system, and we were finally truly in the clear.

We could not have anticipated any of this, but we were lucky to have private health cover in place, which saved us an estimated $58 000 in private hospital fees.

Mentally, perspective was our secret weapon. We literally had to abandon all plans and any sense of control and roll with what came our way. We had to make decisions daily, knowing that the next day would be filled with new decisions that we had no ability to influence. This taught us that no matter what situations come your way, you always have the ability to choose how you respond.

# Pandemics

To borrow from Nitya Prakash, 2020 was like looking both ways before you cross the street, then getting hit by an airplane. The best financial adviser in the world could not have predicted the events of that year and their impact on lives around the world in the years that followed. As the stock markets began to crash in February, the instability of the situation began to emerge.

It seemed like everyone was living their own personal version of Supermarket Sweep meets the movie *Castaway*, but of course pandemic hell was more disastrous for some than it was for others. Deep loss was felt globally as sickness and deaths mounted. Anxiety levels were through the roof, permeating even the most resilient of us. For some, the financial impacts included the loss of jobs and businesses, and in some fields it was no longer possible to earn an income at all. At the same time, for others, the pandemic offered a weird way to squirrel away money that could no longer be spent. Gone were the nights out, the restaurant dining, the holidays. Even hair and beauty got the chop, though online purchases were on the rise.

# Protection

The metaphorical road to Sufficient Funds will have a few, perhaps many, potholes. At times you'll be cruising on the freeway; at others your wheels will be spinning in the sand. Some will be completely wiped off the road by a landslide, avalanche, flood or earthquake. You may be prevented from working, and earning, by serious illness or injury. In such a circumstance, how long could you survive financially without selling everything you own? Pause for a minute to think about this.

For most people, once sick leave and any emergency fund runs out, not being able to work stops their financial plan dead in its tracks, and will likely lead to their selling assets and/or having to survive on insufficient government assistance. This is not your answer and neither is it a sound protection plan.

There's always self-insurance, right? Definitely. For some.

For me, being self-insured means having passive income from investments or a business that can continue to run without you, either of which will pay your living costs for the rest of your life. This might sound a little dramatic, but as financial advisers who do a lot of work in the insurance space, we've seen it all and know this not-at-all-sexy part of your financial plan is absolutely key. Remember what we covered in the previous chapter. Any investment you make is linked specifically to something that truly matters in your quest for Sufficient Funds. Your protection plan should be built around not having to sell these assets (read: give up on your goals) for what is hopefully only a blip on the radar in the grand scheme of your life.

What you need is something to kick in that will save you from having to sell assets, because accident or illness necessitates expensive medical care and/or significant time off work.

One of the best ways to protect your future self from the financial distress that can arise from events like these is having enough insurance to call on if and when needed. If health and lifestyle history allow, and if they are able to factor a manageable premium into their budget, we advise our clients to take out four different types of cover. Payments can generally be split between a rollover from their super fund and a monthly or annual premium from the bank account. Then they can move on with living their epic lives.

Following are the four types of cover you should be considering and what you should factor in when putting them in place.

# Life (aka death) insurance

This pays out a lump sum when you die or are terminally ill. The money goes to whoever you nominate as the beneficiary, or beneficiaries, of your policy. This can help your family continue to cover the bills and living expenses when you die.

You might want to cover:

- medical, legal and funeral costs

- paying out all debt, including mortgage(s)

- leaving a surviving spouse and any dependants with sufficient funds to enable them to at least get back on their feet, or to cover some or all future costs

- larger future costs, such as private school fees.

# TPD insurance

Total and permanent disability insurance is a lump sum paid if an accident or illness means you are unlikely to return to work ever.

TPD really sucks. Financially speaking it's worse than death. This is because you'll never work or earn money again but you need to be kept alive.

Examples of what you might want to cover include:

- any outstanding debt

- income support

- enough to purchase a home outright, if you don't already own one

- payment for an in-home carer or a nanny; an alternative might be your partner, but in that case you will need to replace some of their income

- tax, if the policy is owned and paid for by superannuation, as TPD is a taxable benefit if paid out through your super fund.

## Trauma insurance

This pays you a lump sum when you are diagnosed with a specific illness, including cancer, heart attack or stroke. For young people the most common by far is cancer. Trauma insurance can help support you and your family and pay for medical or rehabilitation costs.

Examples of specifics you might want to cover include:

- your choice of doctor, and travel to enable you to access the best care available. I've seen someone need to travel to the United States for care and return with a US$200 000 medical bill. Private health and Medicare won't cover this.

- income replacement, either for you if your income protection doesn't pay (a doctor says you can still work, even though it's the last thing you'd like to be doing), or if you are unable to obtain income protection

- income support for your partner or someone else who may need to take family time to deal with your trauma.

# Income protection insurance

This pays you a portion of your income if you have an accident or suddenly fall ill. It is paid to you monthly as taxable income, which generally makes premiums tax deductible. This cover is usually the most expensive of all, because it is the most commonly claimed. It is also the most important.

Table 4.2 provides some additional information and rules for different types of cover, including whether your super fund can pay for it. Note these are averages for our clients and certainly not to be taken as personal advice. You need to calculate your specific needs when it comes to each cover type.

### Table 4.2: life insurance structure, tax and premiums

|  | Can my super fund pay for this? | Is it tax deductible to me personally? | Average policy held by clients in the 2023 financial year | Average annual premium |
|---|---|---|---|---|
| Life | Yes | No | $1 375 429 | $836 |
| TPD | Yes | No | $1 538 995 | $1476 |
| Trauma | No | No | $172 489 | $659 |
| Income protection | Yes | Yes | $6670 per month (70% to 80% of gross income) | $2018 |

This is one of the most complex of all personal financial product types, which means it's an absolute minefield and a fairly treacherous DIY adventure should you seek it out.

If you rely on your income and want to avoid being a drain on those around you should something go wrong, discuss your options with a financial adviser. They can help you factor these costs into your budget and give you some peace of mind that, should the worst happen, all will be okay financially.

Here are a few other questions we're commonly asked:

## WHAT IF I ALREADY HAVE INSURANCE WITHIN MY SUPER FUND?

Unless you've applied directly to your super fund to increase your cover, it's likely you will have their default cover and that it will be nowhere near the levels shown in the table above. The risk here, for example, is that you are TPD'd and you have maybe $300 000 total cover. This gives you seven years on Australia's minimum full-time wage, or three years at best if you need a full-time carer and don't meet the myriad requirements to qualify for any type of disability support.

It's an okay fallback, but doesn't take into consideration your personal circumstances or needs. It mightn't, for example, be enough to support your family or to cover expenses in the event of your death.

Also, certain types of insurance are not available through super, such as trauma insurance.

## DO I HAVE TO HAVE A MEDICAL EXAM TO GET INSURANCE?

That depends on your personal health and family history. One of the forms we send clients helps us learn more about their health. From this we can get an idea whether or not a potential insurer might ask for reports from your doctor or require specific tests.

If you have a fairly clear personal medical history and no family history of, say, hereditary illnesses, you might not be required to provide any further information or test results.

## WHAT IF I HAVE PRE-EXISTING HEALTH CONDITIONS? CAN I STILL GET COVER?

Each insurer has their own list of items they will and won't cover. We can do some research for our clients to see whether there are insurers that might cover them despite a pre-existing condition; in most cases we help them find cover with an exclusion or added loading (higher premium) that offsets this risk.

# Dot the i's and cross the t's: your estate plan

In our work with clients, we surround ourselves with teams of professionals to ensure our clients are looked after in every aspect of financial planning. Estate planning is another crucial step in defending your stacks, and you'll need to work with a good solicitor.

Everyone should have both a Will and a power of attorney in place.

A Will is a legally binding document that stipulates how your money and other assets will be split and transferred when you kick the bucket.

A power of attorney, in its various forms, allows someone you trust to make important decisions on your behalf if you are incapacitated.

Everyone knows someone who's had some sort of family drama around wills and the contested distribution of assets. The worst-case scenario sees funds being wasted on legal fees to sort out unnecessary conflicts.

Here are two key steps to avoid this:

1.  Make sure your Will is indeed legally binding. Don't use cheap online Will kits. Spend the money and have your Will drawn up by an experienced solicitor.

2.  Be transparent. If you can, have clear, open conversations with your family (and friends where applicable) to let them know your intentions *before* you die. This could save a heap of confusion as well as wasted time, energy, bad blood and money.

# Did somebody say intergenerational wealth transfer?

Baby boomers are beginning to check out (out of the workforce, that is), and since they are the wealthiest generation in Australian history, over the next few years a whopping $3.5 trillion will be passed down to their kids, who are predominantly Millennials.

There was a time when inheritances were transferred only once older relatives died but there is a growing trend for boomers to pass on some of their assets before they die. This means they may be around to see their beneficiaries rejoice!

The key to the success of this earlier wealth transfer is clear communication and education. Boomers need to be open about their assets and ensure they have a Will in place that details their wishes (simple advice, but too many aren't doing this!). And Millennials need to be asking the right questions, including:

- How will the wealth be transferred and in what form (for example cash, shares or property)?

- How much will be transferred?

- When will it be transferred?

- Who gets Nanna's collection of 84 porcelain elephant statues?

In other words, what has been taboo and unspoken needs to be acceptable and transparent! Both the givers and the recipients should seek solid financial advice about the intricacies of wealth transfer and how to manage the tax implications. Ultimately, this means more of the givers' hard-earned funds end up, as intended, in their kids' hands.

## Sufficiently Defended

Chapter 2 discussed the ins and outs of your funds; now you're across the ups and downs of planning your financial future.

By the end of this chapter:

- ■ You know that a time will come when you'll need to access your emergency fund and you're prepared for the necessary shift in mindset that will require.

- You're prepped for potential life changes. If kids are on the cards, you know how to add them to the balance sheet and are aware of what funds you will need for all stages of starting and growing your family.

- If you face fertility issues, you now understand the money aspects of this journey and you know how to establish funds around this for peace of mind. If you didn't know it before, you know now that you're not alone.

- You've considered how long you could survive financially were you to become sick or to suffer an injury that prevented your working for the foreseeable future.

- You know the types of insurance available, including life insurance, TPD, trauma and income protection, and you understand how crucial these are, at least until you've achieved full financial freedom.

- You have thought about your own Will, but you also have a good idea of whether intergenerational wealth is likely coming in hot! If so, you are equipping yourself with the knowledge you will need to manage the funds. In the interest of transparency, you are sharing what you have learned with your parents and/or siblings. (*Hint*: they could benefit from this book too!)

You are now in the solid position of not only understanding the ins and outs of your money and when and how to invest for growth, but also knowing how to fortify your funds so you can make it through the inevitable ups and downs of the rollercoaster ride that is being alive! Take a deep breath. You're now well on your way to Sufficient Funds.

# CHAPTER FIVE
# Deliver—let it flow

Let's recap your journey to Sufficient Funds. If you've read this far you've defined what's most meaningful to you, and you've aligned your time, energy and money to that end. You've set yourself up for growth and learned how to defend your goals and your money stacks. If you've gone ahead and implemented all of this, it's safe to say you understand what Sufficient Funds means for you and you're on your way to achieving it.

But what's next?

This chapter is about the importance of commitment. It's about staying the course, staying true to yourself, keeping motivated and regularly tweaking your definition of Sufficient Funds.

# Stay the course

Two of the most critical components needed to achieve your Sufficient life are (a) having an awesome plan and (b) sticking to it. Commitment to your plan is just as important as the plan itself. Cruise control (chapter 2) will get you most of the way, but the human factor can creep in — this is essentially you getting in your own damn way.

There are a few tips I share with clients around how to avoid getting in their own way, including making sure any plans have really clear timeframes. If you want to have bought a house by a certain date, write it down, say it out loud. If you want to hold onto an investment for long-term growth and are prepared to ride the waves of the share market or the property market, stay the course and don't be spooked and jump out if you don't absolutely need to.

The other key tip is having an accountability buddy. When we're talking finances this is usually a partner, sometimes a parent or sibling. Whoever this is for you, you'll need to be willing to share your financial details and your plans. I also suggest sharing upfront what you want your buddy to be spotting you for. Whether it's excessive online shopping that could put a dent in your spending plan, or being a bit too loose on the reno budget that could see your investment property returns deflate, they need to know what you are capable of when it comes to sabotaging your own finances.

Another question I ask my clients is: on a scale of 1–10 how committed are you to achieving these goals? There's power in articulating your answer, and if it's less than 9, it's time to take a good hard look at your priorities.

# Stay authentic

Your definition of Sufficient Funds needs to remain authentic. As time goes by you may be tempted to look over your neighbour's fence and confuse one of their assets or achievements with something on your list of priorities. This is one of those times when emotion can override reason and the best way to stay grounded and keep your head on straight is to go back to your definition of Sufficient, and remember that it was built with your unique goals for your authentic self.

It's not always easy being me, or you. Well, at least not until we truly figure it out and embrace it. In today's online world it's way too easy to compare yourself with everyone else and forget who you really are. It's too easy to be lured into the trap of 'fake it till you make it', when it's true authenticity that is your competitive advantage as well as your key to living a fulfilled life.

Once you find true authenticity you have a more accurate compass for living your ideal life. But simply telling someone to be authentic is not actionable advice, as it's rarely that simple. As professional snowboarder Travis Rice puts it, 'If we want authenticity, we have to initiate it. Self-discovery takes us to the wildest places on earth.'

I struggled for a long time to find myself. School for me was about doing anything to fit in. For the most part I was being the person I thought everyone else would appreciate. Sound familiar? It was a comfortable default mode. As a young person it's not always easy to find yourself, so I want to share a few lessons I've learned on this ride so far.

# Trust yourself

You are unique. No one else in the world has your exact set of skills, values and strengths. Your key now is to find these and amplify them.

# Express yourself

Anyone who has met me in the past decade doesn't usually believe this, but I was very quiet at school. My mates in high school used to joke around telling me to shut up, because I was so quiet. I slowly forced myself out of my comfort zone and realised that I had a lot to share.

One of my jobs at uni was selling wine by telemarketing. If you want to learn how to express yourself and build a thick skin at the same time, try cold-calling random people to talk about something you know very little about, with the goal of having them hand over their credit card.

My first financial planning job involved sitting in front of people who had been cold-called and convince them of the benefits of getting help with their money. Before anyone wants to talk about money, they have to be able to trust the person they're talking to. If I didn't come with honesty or true authenticity, I had no chance.

You learn a lot about others but also about yourself in this kind of situation. My EQ developed as I came to better understand the value of what I did as a professional as well as who I was as a person. I also learned a lot about the problems people have with understanding and dealing with money, which is exactly why we built Sufficient Funds.

## Know your worth and stay true to it

Where does the money fit? The net-worth and self-worth balance sheet is an important consideration. For some, as you've defined what Sufficient Funds look like for you, mad stacks are a critical element. For others, knowing you've prioritised aspects of your life that have less to do with money is key.

Net worth is the amount by which your assets exceed your liabilities — your monetary value. Self-worth, on the other hand, is your sense of your own value as a person — think self-esteem or self-respect. Factors that affect your sense of self-worth are strongly linked to what you value in life. They are many and varied for all of us but can include the work you do, your mental and physical health and wellbeing, your relationships, and your sense of purpose.

Prioritising net worth or self-worth is different for everyone. Different cultures place a higher importance on one or the other but even within your family, individuals will be positioned along the net worth to self-worth continuum.

There is no right or wrong place to be on this continuum, but along the way you may, for example, find yourself with more or less money than you'd planned to have, and keeping a focus on staying true to yourself may help keep you on the right track.

## Get real

Take a moment to run through your goals and make sure these are *your* goals. It's so important to make sure you're living your life for you. It's not about comparing your life with those of others or setting goals because that's what you think you *should* be doing. Identify your core values and make sure your plans align with them.

The only way you will be truly happy is if you can look back at your achievements and know they reflect your true authentic self, they were meaningful to you and you made them happen.

# Find a Sufficient cause and make a difference that counts

I'm hoping that while reading this book you've spent a lot of time thinking about yourself and your personal situation. It's like the air-emergency rule: fit your own oxygen mask first. Now you can think more broadly about how you can truly make a difference to others.

For many people I meet every day, 'being the change you want to see in the world' is more than just an empty mantra. It's a way of life. Giving and giving back are concepts they want to include in their weekly or monthly spending plans and, when it comes to time commitments, their calendars. Others will have a strong desire to share wealth by donating to charity. Don't think you have to put this off until you've reached a point where you have excess funds — for example, once you've hit a salary of $150 000, or once you've paid off 75 per cent of your mortgage. As I hope I've shown you in this book, income or asset targets are rarely a good indicator of when you're ready for a certain action. It may be you could start smaller but sooner, then increase your donations as your budget or asset position allows. There are no simple answers here; it all comes down to your unique set of values and the drive you have to make a difference.

When I started out in financial planning, I had no idea of the impact I would make on clients — perfect strangers tapping into our service — but also on my nearest and dearest. I've been able to help friends and relatives buy their first home, set themselves up for retirement and plan for time off work as they've expanded their families. The pure joy I get from this is a huge reward for me and makes each and every day I work on my business significant for me.

Is making a difference to someone other than yourself one of your key goals? If so, I want to show you how to implement two simple steps to feel Sufficient in this space:

- Identify the cause or causes that really matter to you.

- Set up a regular savings plan to ensure you not only *think* about donating your hard-earned to the right cause, but you actually *do* it!

When it comes to identifying the cause or the direction of donations, it can be useful to think broadly about why you wish to add donations to your overall plans for Sufficient Funds. The following are overarching themes I see with my clients:

- *Make it truly meaningful.* Let's face it, when it comes to justifying the hours we spend behind our laptops, commuting (for those who still do) and sacrificing time beyond the 9 to 5, we want to know that we are making decisions and trade-offs in exchange for something meaningful. Some people place value on making a positive difference in the world, finding meaning in their actions beyond money-oriented success, and they prioritise

philanthropy and social impact as a way to contribute to a
higher purpose, something greater than themselves.

- *Align your giving with your clearly defined values and beliefs.*
  This is particularly true for those I see who are passionate
  about causes like global warming and climate justice,
  equality and human rights. These issues ignite a passion,
  and the ability to channel funds towards advancing these
  causes can be highly motivating. Giving to organisations
  that support these values, with either time or money, can
  mean making a change for the greater good — one person,
  one hour, one dollar at a time.

- *Empathy runs deep.* For many, especially Millennials and
  GenZ, a strong sense of empathy and deep connection are
  highly important catalysts linking intention and action. This
  includes being acutely aware of those issues impacting all of
  humanity. It also includes a need to not live this life on a solo
  mission that is driven by self-benefit and stacking up assets,
  Scrooge McDuck–style. The sense of responsibility, the desire
  to give to those less fortunate, is absolute and non-negotiable.

- *Work, but do it for cause.* Many people are increasingly
  keen to align their careers with organisations that are doing
  good work in the world. The rise of job candidates seeking
  roles where they can be assured the organisation is socially
  responsible and aligns philanthropy with its company
  mission and values has led many companies to double down
  in this space. The bonus here is you can be giving back
  while you're on the job, and in many cases doubling money
  contributions to charities for which employers offer dollar-
  matching fundraising donations.

- *Influencers for good.* Social media and digital tech have played a huge role in shaping an interconnected and socially conscious world. Information at our fingertips has made us more attuned to humanitarian challenges and more connected to platforms and digital mechanisms for raising awareness, amplifying messages and mobilising voluntary action in response to influencer stimuli.

Nowadays, charitable donations take a range of forms. You may still be approached by old-school door-knockers and cold-callers, and now a range of digital platforms can easily be shared or linked through social media. This means that when it comes to making decisions around donations, it can be hard to think purposefully through all that noise. With more and more choices for where to send your extra cash it can be hard to keep track of your donations. In many cases donations are tax-deductible, but it's easy to get caught up in the idea of donating for donating's sake and in the process spread your funds so thinly they lose any meaning or efficacy.

When you donate to a charitable cause, use the same decision-making process you do any time you spend money. Take the time to pause and donate with purpose.

---

**Note:** You will recall from chapter 3 that tax deductibility alone gets far more airplay than it deserves and should only ever be viewed as a side-benefit of something you are planning to do anyway. Never decide to do something just because it's tax deductible. It varies depending on your tax rate, but it's like dropping a dollar to pick up 30 cents. The only way it makes sense here is when it's directed to a cause that truly matters.

---

Where possible, when identifying the cause, keep it streamlined and simple. Make a conscious decision to support one or two that have true meaning for you, rather than a handful that you don't necessarily align with. Either way make sure it is a conscious decision.

For some it's a no-brainer; for others it's a more considered choice. You might feel pressure to choose the 'right' cause or to be able to explain why you chose it. If you find yourself in a spin, here are my top tips for identifying your cause. You may be able to clarify your philanthropic goals, identify your priorities, and make well-informed decisions on aligning your donations with your values and your definition of Sufficient Funds. Ask yourself the following questions (if you have a parent approaching a time when they are considering where to transfer their wealth, and they want to include charity as well as family, these questions might help with that conversation):

- *What cause do I want to look back on in 10 years' time and feel I was right to support it?*

- *Do I want to support something in my own backyard or would I prefer to make a difference to a national or global issue?*

- *How soon do I want to be able to see the impact?* Do I prefer to support immediate relief efforts, long-term systemic change or perhaps a combination of both?

- *Do I need to see the results of my donations to motivate me to save more for this cause?* Reflect on the issues that personally resonate and will drive savings in line with your core values. Does the mission of a particular organisation

resonate on an emotional level so I feel motivated to
support their work wholeheartedly?

- *Do I prefer to help a stranger or someone I know?* (No
one said you have to donate to an organisation; it may be
much more meaningful to you if you can personally see
the impact.)

- *Do I want to contribute to a variety of causes?*

- *Is it important to me that the charity has good standing so
I can be confident my dollars end up where they will really
count?* If transparency and accountability are key, check
out choice.com.au for a charity checklist and how to avoid
being scammed. You can do your own research by checking
out an organisation's publicly available info. Look for details
on how they allocate funds, how they measure impact, and
how they report their results. Do they share evidence of
regular audits and financial info (as all nonprofits should)?

- *An organisation may be reputable, but how efficiently and
effectively do they deploy your donations?* You could do a
deeper dive and compare their admin expenses and their
program expenses. Do they have a proven record of effective
programs and initiatives? Ideally you'll want to donate to
organisations who invest a significant chunk of their budget
directly into programs rather than into admin costs.

- *How can my donation have the greatest impact?* Sometimes
a few bucks here or there can feel like it won't make much
difference to the big causes. A little bit of research can help
you find opportunities that extend your donations, such as

dollar-matching initiatives, in which a wealthy individual or corporate organisation offers to match each donation. Or think about collaborating with friends or colleagues to give together to make a bigger impact.

- *Do I have the capacity to contribute more than money?* Depending on the organisation, you may be able to contribute your time and skills towards volunteer efforts, or pro-bono work.

- *Do I want to establish a long-term donation plan?* Do I want to make this a one-off donation or am I happy to have recurring donations direct debited?

# Set up a regular donations plan

Okay, so you've made your decisions and know what cause or causes you want to focus on. Now there are some logistics to figure out. My list of top questions to ask includes the following:

- *How much do you want to donate?*

- *Do you want to direct debit?* As with savings in general (chapter 2), if you don't automate it and allocate funds before they hit the spending account, will it really happen? Even better, do you have pre-tax options through your employer?

- *Do you want to make a one-off annual payment or regular payments throughout the year?* This will depend on your individual cash flow. For example, if you receive an annual bonus, would it be easier if your contribution came at this time of year?

- *Have you thought about saving over a longer period — a number of months or years — before making a significant contribution?*

Whatever your answers, stay true to what drives you and your definition of Sufficient Funds.

# Keep motivated

Staying the course and staying true to yourself sound great, but they will absolutely take energy and require you to stay motivated around your goals, your plans and your definition of Sufficient.

Don't expect motivation and encouragement to just show up when you need it. You may have heard the line about it being too late to build a relationship when you need one. The same is true for building a source of motivation. So, in an era when motivation is everywhere but you need to hit 'Subscribe' when it counts, here are my recommendations for how to best channel the good energy and make it work for you.

## Curate your content

The information you feed yourself will have an impact on you. The information you invite into your life each day shapes your world, your thoughts and, eventually, your decisions. These days you have so many opportunities to allow content to enter your brain space.

Sure, it can be debated that data-led marketing is pushing content at you at a rate of knots, but there are still many ways you can curate what you're opting into. Whether it's your socials, the podcasts you listen to, the books you read or, IRL, the company you keep. No matter your source of information, it can be a source of motivation, so make sure it aligns with your goals and the elements that make up your definition of Sufficient. There are apps that help you unsubscribe from emails and other content that isn't aligned to your needs, while I encourage you to actively lean in to those sources that do align. Scroll through your social apps and opt in to anything that delivers information that positively aligns with the direction in which you're headed.

## Find your motivator

I have spent my entire working life helping people figure out their money stuff to achieve their goals. This is what makes me tick! But even when it comes so naturally, sometimes I still need to find the motivation.

Your motivator could be your partner, a close friend or family member, a mentor or colleague. If you have such a person, hold on to them tightly. If it is someone lifting you up in each and every conversation you have, you've hit the jackpot and all I can say is you'd better be giving back as much as you get because that's a relationship you want to hang onto. However, not everyone (probably not even most people) can turn to such a person, for two simple reasons: people hate talking about money, and it scares them to reveal too much even to their nearest and dearest.

In Australia, we also have this really annoying knack of cutting down tall poppies. Everyone is looking over the fence at the Joneses.

As soon as they start achieving big things there's suddenly a target on their backs. Makes heaps of sense, right?

These are my three key takeaways for helping you find a motivator:

1. **Share.** Share your money situation, your goals and your definition of Sufficient Funds. Encourage those around you to do the same, and assuming you find someone willing to open up, over time you might just find yourself an accountability buddy and someone who pumps you up and keeps you looking ahead!

2. **Go mentor hunting.** Actively seek out a mentor. If you're lucky, you'll already have the benefit of such a person in your work life, but if not, think about setting out one or two of your key goals. Find someone just beyond your circle to reach out to, and ask them if they would be willing to be a mentor. As my kids tell me, if you don't ask, you don't get, so you need to get comfortable asking, which means getting comfortable about articulating your goals. And think of your circle *as* a circle. You're not necessarily looking for someone older, or someone who's above you in career terms or in terms of financial success. Think about those who are one step across and one step below (sometimes termed reverse mentoring). It's naive to think that you can't be motivated by someone just because they aren't already more successful than you. And finally, commit. Don't stand them up, be gracious and grateful, and when it comes time for someone to hit you up, pay it back in spades!

3. **Don't stress if you don't have someone in real life.** We are absolutely surrounded by energising sources of

influence, from famous motivational speakers to successful business achievers to the resonant TikTok or Insta influencer. Find someone, or something, that resonates and subscribe! Again, automating is key. If you have this person pop up on your social feed during your morning coffee without even having to search, you are using social media marketing to your advantage.

Whatever your motivator, you need to call on it regularly. Whether it's a chat with a friend or mentor, a flick through realestate.com for your ideal location, a quick squiz at the latest Flight Centre deals or some Insta inspo, find what stokes your fire and turn it up!

The only way you're going to achieve your goals is by summoning the necessary energy and enthusiasm. Go!

# Redefine Sufficient

Hopefully you have now spent a lot of time and energy shaping your definition of Sufficient, but remember it's not a static concept. From time to time, depending on what's going on in your life and in the world around you, you will need to review and update that definition.

A good starting point is to revisit chapter 1 to ensure you haven't missed anything or let a few old habits creep back in. Remember that you set your definition of what a fulfilling and successful life looked like for you. But I also cautioned that this was going to be done to the 'best of your ability' at that point in time with your current mindset. Perspectives shift and we can only see so far ahead. This is revealed to me over and over again in the work we do with clients.

We have three sessions with new clients leading up to when they start to implement their Money Action Plan (MAP)™. Sessions are usually about four to six weeks apart. We define 'Sufficient' in the first one, then revisit it and dive deeper in the second. I can tell you that when the second session comes around and we're revisiting the goals and values set in the first, something is *always* added in, taken away or significantly updated — *and it's only been a month!* Twelve months on, you're likely to see some significant changes.

There's so much of life to be lived beyond Sufficient Funds. This is where the real magic happens. Everything is flowing for you and you're starting to build mad momentum. This is the point at which you may be ready to work towards what we define as Beyond Sufficient.

Here are some of the prompts we use with our clients when we revisit their definition of Sufficient Funds to make sure their Money Action Plan (MAP)™ continues to deliver on what matters to them:

- *You've achieved epic milestones.* Time to celebrate, if you haven't already! You got married, turned your side-hustle into a full-time gig, bought the house near the beach, got the sweet new EV, reached Mt Everest base camp (as a few of our clients did this year), started a family, graduated with an MBA. The list goes on and on, so revisit your original list from chapter 1 and make the updates.

- *You've experienced a shift in your health or wellbeing.* Evaluate any updates in your own wellbeing. How are you feeling generally? Any new health issues, or a problem you've managed to overcome or move out of your life? Did you start a new PT regime that is costing a bomb but has been a total lifesaver? I started getting into yoga — shoutout to my teacher, Louisa, from Lunge! Louisa effortlessly makes the connection between the work you're doing in class and the associated benefits to your body and mind. I also started to learn more about the benefits of healthy eating in conjunction with a good exercise routine, and suddenly I was eating a lot more wholefoods and cutting out a heap of sugar — cue the upgraded grocery budget!

- *You've started a new hobby.* Are you like one of our clients who recently got her helicopter licence? In her first Money Action Plan (MAP)™, this was a costly one-off goal that she planned and saved for, but now she's qualified, she has to factor a whole new cost into her Spending Plan to keep her flying and enjoying the fruits of her labour!

  Do you need to free up more time to be able to take on other hobbies you've been putting off? Do you need to evaluate your work hours or how you're spending your weekends in order to do more of this? I juggle surfing and mountain biking, and often find I've let one or the other (sometime both) slip out of the routine. Surfing especially is one of my happy places; it's great for grounding me. Stop and think about hobbies regularly and ensure you're allocating the right amount of time, and money, to keep on top of these valuable pleasures.

- *Your family and relationships change.* How much time did you spend hanging with your besties this year? Have you made the trip you said you would to visit an old friend or distant relative? How many weddings might be coming up this year, and where are they? Consider the evolution of your friendships and relationships with family members. There's always a delicate balance here, but relationships are a strong source of wellbeing, and they need to align with your money plan.

On the family front you may have thought you knew what you wanted your future family to look like, but has this changed? Can you now see yourself having more kids, fewer kids, are step kids now in the picture? Is the timing and process of starting a family now looking a little different from the way it did when you first defined it?

- *Your enthusiasm for your current line of work has changed.* Feeling stagnant at work? Perhaps a career change or a new business is on the cards? Are you keen to explore and develop your public speaking skills, or is it time to enrol in a new course that will help you get the next big promotion at work? Or have you graduated and sworn that you'll never pick up another textbook in your life? Guess what, you now have a heap of free time. How are you going to use it?

- *Your desire to give back dials up a notch.* I discussed this at length earlier in this chapter so you can refer to this as you review how your current actions and financial plan support your philanthropic goals and desire for social impact.

As you learn and grow through life your perspectives shift and your priorities change. With charities you might set up a direct debit that runs monthly and becomes set and forget. (Great automation! See chapter 2.) However, just like your 14 streaming services, these can easily be forgotten, and since your resources for giving are likely to be finite it's important the causes you still really care about are the ones receiving your hard-earned.

- *You want to shift the scales of work–life integration.* Remember, a key element of achieving Sufficient Funds isn't about stopping work forever; it's about enjoying the work you do so you don't feel the need to escape it. So work–life balance becomes more about integration. Are you still enjoying the work you're doing? Are you getting enough time outside of work to explore other joys in life?

  It may seem like a pipe dream to take a break from work or to shift from full-time to part-time in order to align the way you spend the time you have and your values, but at some point, when you can see your finances looking a little more chunky, and your confidence creeps up, you may have a different perspective on how you want to spend your days.

  It's a constant juggling act, and we have regular conversations with our clients around ensuring that their Money Action Plan (MAP)™ continues to link back to their highest priorities. If you get this right, everything flows and life is good.

- *You need to turn to a contingency plan.* This means your emergency fund (chapter 2) or your life and income protection insurances (chapter 4). Did you have to use your emergency fund and wish it had been larger? Experience guides our future decisions so a mishap can often lead to a better decision next time. Your appetite for risk can change temporarily or more permanently.

Did some extra funds sneak into your emergency fund as you forgot to stop when you reached your ideal number? These funds can now be reallocated. After we reviewed ours recently we cut the emergency fund by 25 per cent as we realised we were being overly cautious. We invested those funds instead, and we're now $15k better off due to this tweak. It's nice when things play out like this.

- *You have new experiences.* Do you have the experience vs things balance right (chapter 1)? What have you been able to tick off that list? How did it make you feel? Do you need to do more of the things you've been enjoying, or is there something else that needs to be added now?

There are significant benefits to prioritising experiences in your life. You create lasting memories, whether with a significant other, your young family, or just a meaningful memory that will stay with you personally as you navigate the rollercoaster of life.

One of the biggies in this category is travel. There's a reason we refer to the 'travel bug' — it's contagious and hard to shake. Travel expands your world and that experience can feed the desire to continue to explore. So someone who has been comfortable with a yearly interstate trip but visited Europe for the first time in the post-pandemic European summer craze, may just discover they now have three other trips they'd *love* to take in the next two or three years. Time to upgrade that savings plan and channel more cash to this epic goal!

Tash and I value travelling to new places, locally and internationally, with our young kids. We believe there is huge value in this for them. Even if they don't remember much, it still expands their world and their comfort zones so it's a priority in our lives. We also love going back to places we've visited in the past and creating new memories there.

# Isn't financial advice just for old people who already have mad stacks?

So what does a financial adviser actually do? Our young clients come to us for many reasons. Following are some of these:

- You have money left over after each pay and you're trying to decide where it should go. You may have an overarching goal of paying down the mortgage, for example, but have you considered how investing these funds would impact your financial position? What about benefiting from 30+ years of compound returns inside super?

- You spend what seems like a lot on things most people save up for, but that's chill because you get paid again next week. This is a sure-fire predictor of major regret in a few years' time, when you stop and look back at your massive cumulative income and wonder where it all went. You know you should be keeping more of what you're earning, and now you've read the book you can see it's possible, but if you had someone holding your hand through the process it would be far more effective than DIY.

- You're a first home buyer and you're wondering how much mortgage is too much, especially as the apartment you're about to buy might only work for child one, but you're not sure what impact income fluctuations will have as you balance starting a family with the likely need to upgrade the home again in five years' time when child two may be on their way.

- You want to know you're putting the right proportion of your resources into each of the four stacks of Sufficient Funds. Remember from chapter 3 that this involves careful decisions around your approach to debt, savings, investment and super. The only way to ensure you're contributing to the right stacks at the right time is to map out your life over a number of years so you can understand the impact of the infinite variations that will impact your plan (chapter 1). This means you will not only understand the impact your money decisions will have, but also ensure you remain on track as you make the many ongoing changes and tweaks that will be required over time.

- You are dealing with moving pieces. You're juggling work fluctuations (babies, mini-retirements), education funding, big purchases (can I get the EV?).

- You are at a crossroads. Perhaps you've already got the house, but you've got extra funds, so where to from here?

- You've received an inheritance (see chapter 4).

Now, some of these situations may not require you to engage a financial adviser and, indeed, given you've chosen to read this book you may be well on your way to effectively managing your own finances. Nonetheless, it may still be a good idea to seek input from a professional for these reasons:

- **Expertise** *(We're self-admitted money nerds).* Financial advisers are qualified professionals with expertise in many aspects of personal finance. We have a deep understanding of investment, super, tax and insurance strategies and can help you wade through the associated minefields!

- **Access to tools, resources and platforms** *(We've got the goods).* We have access to a world of sophisticated software, analysis and projection tools and other resources that are exclusively for professional use. Utilising these allows us to build a Money Action Plan (MAP)™ that gives you full insight into the future impact of current financial decisions.

- **Holistic approach** *(We do life and money).* We take into consideration your entire money and life situation including personal goals and risk tolerance, and money aspects such as your budget, savings, investments, tax planning and retirement requirements. From this a financial plan can be created that ensures all of the above aspects are integrated into a comprehensive strategy.

- **Coaching and behavioural guidance** *(We've got your back!).* We're all about epic, genuine relationships. As I'm sure you've gathered by this point in the book, financial planning for us is about way more than money. Having someone relatable, with high emotional intelligence, coach you through the conversations you need to have around your life and the intertwined monetary aspects is crucial. This is so important during the inevitable ups and downs. When it comes to making rational and sometimes emotional money decisions, a financial adviser can provide guidance and help protect you from your own impulsive spending habits and investment decisions.

- **On track with your stacks** *(We're your accountability buddy)*. We all need someone to keep us on track, and a financial adviser is an expert in this space. Support through regular meetings and check-ins can help you stay the course and make timely adjustments to your plan.

- **Regulation and compliance** *(We know, and play by, the rules)*. There are heavy rules that govern how we operate as a profession. A financial adviser is legally obligated to provide advice that is in your best interests.

- **Time saving** *(We've got the time)*. Whether it's researching investment options, analysing market trends and legislation changes, or making sure your Plan is fully actioned (implemented), these activities are highly time consuming. Even for the most money-savvy individuals, having someone take this major responsibility off your plate can free up your time and brainpower to focus on other aspects that meet your definition of Sufficient. You do you, we do money.

# Sufficiently Delivered

You have arrived at Sufficient Funds! Well, at the very least, you're getting close. You've defined exactly what your ideal life looks like and have begun creating and implementing the plan that will make it flow!

- You've worked through Defining, Decluttering, Developing, Defending and Delivering Sufficient Funds for you.

- You have a good understanding of how to stay on track and stay motivated, and how to tackle it all while remaining true to your values as you pursue your personal definition of Sufficient Funds.

- You know that none of this is static, and that the meaning of Sufficient Funds for you will evolve. You're now fully equipped to redefine Sufficient and understand some of the circumstances that will lead you to it.

- You understand when and how to seek professional advice when you need help and guidance along the way.

You're now a long way from Insufficient Funds and are well equipped to bounce yourself right back, should you fall behind or even if you find yourself in that position again. Remember that success is in the journey. You now have all the tools you've built along the way and, *most important*, the confidence to make your funds work for you!

# THINK BIGGER: BEYOND SUFFICIENT

At the beginning of this book I described the helpless feeling associated with Insufficient Funds and how I wanted to transport you as far from that feeling as possible. I mentioned that if you remain in a position of Insufficient Funds for too long, you are likely to have to settle for a less enjoyable life and, ultimately, for being unhappy and completely unfulfilled.

Throughout this book you've been working on defining and setting the wheels in motion on your version of Sufficient. In five chapters we've outlined a clear plan for exactly how you will Define, Declutter, Develop, Defend and Deliver in order to reach Sufficient Funds. Now you can be clear and confident about your future, you have a protection plan and suitable buffers in place and you're building mad stacks in all the areas you need so you can achieve all the big goals you've set for yourself. Life is good!

In chapter 5, I took you through the financial planning process and numerous examples of Redefining Sufficient as you achieve milestones or as shifts occur in your life. Redefining Sufficient will be a constant part of your life and will help ensure you stay motivated and on track. This is a crucial element of being fulfilled. Remember, you're not striving for a permanent recliner beach chair from which to gaze at the horizon. You're seeking constant progress and its associated sense of achievement. This is what brings happiness.

What if it's not all rosy and I stumble or fall?

I want you to accept that life is going to throw you curveballs, and to be prepared when it happens. If you've carefully followed each of the chapters in sequence, you should be as financially prepared as you possibly can be. Of course this won't eliminate the emotional toll resulting from an unanticipated event such as a death in the family, a medical emergency or a business collapse, and this is where building a strong support network around you can help.

Here is our vision for what our clients will achieve:

*They will define, achieve and reach beyond Sufficient Funds. They will have the confidence and clarity to create a lifelong shift from hopes and dreams to reality. They will create abundant wealth, and have the time and health to enjoy it.*

The key here is the reach. The stretch. I want you not only to achieve Sufficient, but to reach beyond Sufficient towards Abundance. In chapter 1, I proposed that your goals need to be big enough to give you the motivation to chase them down. As Richard Branson once said, 'If people aren't calling you crazy, you aren't thinking big enough.' Remaining on track is one thing, but constantly pushing your limits and challenging yourself to think bigger is a whole different ball game.

If you think about achieving Sufficient Funds as reaching Everest base camp, Beyond Sufficient means summiting the mountain. Pushing your thoughts beyond your original definition of Sufficient will not only motivate you to stay on track; it will increase your chances of achieving those initial goals and more.

This is often where the original list of goals for five years, 10 years and beyond becomes a serious focus. You've nailed all the small stuff — now it's time to really dream.

In money terms, don't focus on what your stacks will look like at the end of the month, the quarter or even the year. What does Sufficient Funds look like for you in 10 or 20 years' time? Think about those big life goals; give yourself permission to dream and get set to smash them.

This is where it gets really wide and varied. To get you thinking, here's a short list of life goals from our clients as well as from our own experience:

- Full financial freedom, meaning we can choose to never work again without sacrificing lifestyle

- Spending every northern hemisphere winter in a debt-free house in the foothills of powder-mecca Niseko, Japan, with your very own onsen

- Becoming engaged in true philanthropy — for example, setting up a scholarship fund for children in an area where you spent time working many years ago

- Investing serious time and money in business opportunities or charitable pursuits

- Fully kitting out a LandCruiser and camper-trailer for regular family adventures

- Designing and custom building your own home on five acres overlooking the beach or rolling hills

- Funding medical research in an area you've personally had to access so others never have to suffer what you went through

- Venturing into space

- Investing in your own health and wellbeing so you'll benefit from what you have achieved.

Remember, achieving Sufficient is not a goal to apply only to money. I want you to create abundant wealth, yes, but the vision I have for you includes the time and the health to enjoy it. Imagine a world in which money isn't a constraint on your time, and your time isn't a constraint to your health.

Now imagine the new feeling you'd have if this was your reality and how far that feeling is from that dismal message of 'Insufficient Funds' on the ATM slip. Let go of that image, hold onto that new feeling and go smash it!

# GOT STUCK?
# REACH OUT

Hopefully as a result of this book you're now smashing it out of the park. If you get to a point that you need some extra guidance, then please shout. We have a solid team of financial advisers and mortgage brokers who live and breathe this stuff and are stoked to help you out.

Scan the QR code, or head to sufficientfunds.com.au to learn a bit more about us, and to get in touch.

# NOTES

## Chapter 1

*The Tim Ferriss Show* transcripts, episode 56: Peter Diamandis. Show notes and links at tim.blog/podcast.

Calderwood, J 2011, 'Kuwait Gives Each Citizen Dh13000 and free food', *The National News*, 18 January.

## Chapter 2

Ramsey Solutions 2024, https://www.ramseysolutions.com/debt/debt-snowball-vs-debt-avalanche

Clear, James 2018, *Atomic Habits: An Easy and Proven Way to Build Habits and Break Bad Ones*, Penguin Random House.

# Chapter 3

CoreLogic 2022, 'The long game…30 years of housing values', *Property Pulse, Research News,* 29 August.

Bajpai, P 2023, 'Liquidity of Bitcoin', *Investopedia,* https://www .investopedia.com/articles/.

# Chapter 4

Armour, M, Lawson, K, Wood, A, et al. 2019, 'The cost of illness and economic burden of endometriosis and chronic pelvic pain in Australia: A national online survey'. *PLoS ONE* 14(10): e0223316.

Printed and bound by CPI Group (UK) Ltd, Croydon, CR0 4YY

18/06/2024

14516730-0001